THE BUSINESS AND CULTURE OF DIGITAL GAMES

THE BUSINESS AND CULTURE OF DIGITAL GAMES

Gamework/Gameplay

Aphra Kerr

SAGE Publications

London ● Thousand Oaks ● New Delhi

First published 2006

SAGE Publications Ltd
1 Oliver's Yard
55 City Road
London EC1Y 1SP

SAGE Publications Inc.
2455 Teller Road
Thousand Oaks, California 91320

SAGE Publications India Pvt Ltd
B-42, Panchsheel Enclave
Post Box 4109
New Delhi 110 017

British Library Cataloguing in Publication data

A catalogue record for this book is available from the
British Library

ISBN-10 1-4129-0046-8   ISBN-13 978-1-4129-0046-1
ISBN-10 1-4129-0047-6 (pbk)   ISBN-13 978-1-4129-0047-8

Library of Congress Control Number available

Typeset by C&M Digitals (P) Ltd., Chennai, India
Printed in Great Britain by Athenaeum Press, Gateshead
Printed on paper from sustainable resources

CONTENTS

LIST OF TABLES AND FIGURES

TABLES

FIGURES

ACKNOWLEDGEMENTS

I would love to say writing this book has been all play but that would be somewhat misleading! It has certainly been a learning experience, both in terms of my knowledge about this area and in terms of my game playing ability. I doubt that either will finish with this book.

The research which led to this book would not have taken place without the financial support of Dublin City University and the Irish Research Council for the Humanities and Social Sciences. These funding bodies showed faith in the ideas and in me and I hope that this book in some way repays their faith.

A large number of people responded positively to my requests for information and interviews. Many of these people were extremely busy in their own jobs trying to make games and others were willing to meet me in the evening. Your life stories are woven throughout this book and I hope I have done them some justice.

It is difficult to assess how important www.gamedevelopers.ie has been in all this. The website emerged as a kind of action project from the first year of my post-doctorate and grew into a lively community of academics, game players and industry. It spawned face-to-face social events and some more serious events and people on the forum helped me to decide on a name for the book. I owe them a lot more than they can imagine. Special thanks to Tony, Dave, Ian and John; game players, designers, developers, proof readers and friends.

Throughout my postdoctoral research project I have been fortunate enough to have a number of mentors. At the University of Ulster Professor Máire Messenger-Davies encouraged me to finalise the book and gave me time and space to do the work. In my previous position at Dublin City University, Professor Paschal Preston provided both theoretical and practical guidance to help navigate the research and publication processes. Dr Maggie Gibbons provided both professional and personal support. Particular mention needs to be paid to Julian

Kücklich for introducing me to many games, including *Carcasonne*, and for his astute and meticulous editing.

At Sage I would like to thank my editor Julia Hall and Fabienne Pedroletti for patiently and cheerfully answering all my questions and guiding me through the process.

I would also like to thank Betty and John and George and Olive for their unquestioning support, hospitality and love. Go raibh míle maith agaibh.

Finally, a special thanks to my partner John for his patience and support, regardless of the distance. Le grá.

Aphra Kerr

ONE

INTRODUCTION

Digital games are an intrinsic part of contemporary global flows of cultural goods, services and images in Western societies. Developed in parts of Asia, the US, Australia and Europe and played on electronic goods manufactured in cheap labour/low tax economies, they are part and parcel of the global economy. From an economic perspective they are merely commodities, created as cheaply as possible and sold in those markets that are rich enough to afford them. They are no different to, and from, other information goods and services whose value is dependent on what the customer is willing to pay for them. Yet this book argues that they *are* different and that digital games, as a transmedial cultural form, play an important role in reshaping communication patterns, social structures and cultural practice across space and time.

Digital games appear to epitomise an ideal type of global post-industrial neo-liberal cultural product. As products they are based on the innovative fusion of digital technologies and cultural creativity; as a media industry they exploit global networks of production and distribution with little to no regulation; and as a cultural practice they embody the liberal ideals of individual choice and agency. One can play what one wants to play at any time and in any place if one can afford it. As with many research topics, the reality is in fact far more complex. As we shall see, digital games must still attend to local cultural practices, tastes and social structures if they are to succeed across the major markets. This book sets out to establish just how 'global' and 'new' digital games are, and to assess the findings in terms of pre-existing media and social theories.

While traditional media companies and institutions struggle to go digital and exploit 'interactivity', digital games have been digital from the beginning, at least of their commercial existence. Digital games can respond and adapt to the player in ways that make the 'press the red button' interactivity of digital television in the UK pale into insignificance. At the same time, digital games 'remediate', in the sense proposed by Bolter and Grusin (2000) and borrow from television, computers and the internet, to offer new business opportunities, new performance spaces and new experiences to their users. Digital games also encourage their users to become 'authors' and to produce game content which can be circulated and played by other users. However, as with many new technologies, the actual application and exploitation of this technological potential is far from straightforward and uniform.

As with any innovation, digital games are surrounded by both utopic and dystopic discourses. In part these stem from the particular historical moment when digital games developed, i.e. the late 1960s, and in part from the wider social formations in which they are situated, i.e. globalising capitalist democracies. Digital games emerged in an era when discourses of the post-industrial and the post-modern dominated and when existing public regulation of the media and communications institutions was being dismantled. They emerged from a period of large public investment in science programmes, the Space Race and the Cold War and, less obviously perhaps, from widespread civil rights movements and marches. It is perhaps unsurprising that they should at the same time hold out the promise of new spaces for sociality, virtuality and identity construction while also embodying fears about the increasing levels of violence, individualisation and consumption in society.

Many of the hopes and fears attached to digital games are based on speculation and conjecture rather than academic analysis and contextually situated empirical research. There is little in the way of independent statistics on the growth and value of the industry and few large-scale academically rigorous studies of game players and game cultures. The work that has emerged to date from media studies in many ways takes theories developed for the study of the mass media and applies them in the context of computer-mediated communications and peer-to-peer networks. How can we talk with authority about the effects of digital games when we are only beginning to understand the game/user relationship and the degree to which it gives more creative freedom and agency to users? The research that has been conducted points to significant diversity between products, platforms, uses and users. It is time to highlight the limitations of our legacy theories and concepts.

For many digital games are mystifying, challenging and to varying degrees, viewed as dangerous. They are the media 'black box' which, like the home (before audience researchers ventured inside), is misunderstood, feared and surrounded by stereotypes. To the casual onlooker video games are violent, sexist and addictive. The language of lag rates, pinging, fragging and bosses is unintelligible to outsiders and while the console may have made it into many living rooms, it has still to make it into the hearts of older generations and many females, of all ages. This book aims to give the reader a peek inside the black box that is digital games and to contribute to our broader collective understanding of their complexity.

WHY USE THE TERM 'DIGITAL GAMES'?

Many books use a platform-specific term like 'video games' or 'computer games' to refer to the entire field of digital games. These terms are however problematic, given their far from universal application. Herz (1997), Poole (2000: 35) and Wolf (2001: 17), for example, refer to games on arcade machines, consoles and PCs as 'video games'. Cornford et al. (2000) prefer to distinguish between computer and video games, while Haddon (1993) uses the broad term 'interactive games'. Meanwhile, the online academic journal, *Game Studies*, described itself as the 'international journal of computer game research'. As a relatively new field, such definitional differences are not unusual, and indeed may reflect different user cultures since computer games are somewhat more popular in Europe and South East Asia than in the USA and Japan, where video games reign supreme.

This book uses the term 'digital games' to refer to the entire field and to embrace arcade, computer, console and mobile games in all their diversity. Digital games emerged as a useful designation for the field during the formation of the Digital Games Research Association (DIGRA) in 2003. A consensus emerged during lengthy discussions that digital games signalled both the differences and the historical and formal similarities between digital and non-digital games. Indeed, at the inaugural DIGRA conference, Jesper Juul (2003) talked about the transmedial nature of games and highlighted the historical continuities between classical games and digital games. Espen Aarseth (2001), in the inaugural editorial of the journal *Game Studies*, also points to the fact that digital games are 'not one medium, but many different media'.

In the present volume, a digital game could refer to a game played on arcade cabinets, on PC or MAC, on consoles like the PlayStation 2, the GameCube and the Xbox, on mobile devices like mobile phones or over the internet. While digital games are available on a diverse range of platforms, they are fundamentally produced, distributed and exhibited using digital technologies and are composed of what Lev Manovich calls 'numerical representations' (Manovich 2001). This allows digital games to be easily 'ported' from one platform to another. Consequently, in this book PC games and console games will refer to subsectors of the field, while digital games refers to the entire field.

THEORETICAL APPROACH

The underlying premise in this book is that digital games are socially constructed artefacts that emerge from a complex process of negotiation between various human and non-human actors within the context of a particular historical formation. Digital games cannot be understood without attention to the late capitalist economic systems from which they emerge and the changing political, social and cultural contexts in which they are produced and consumed. This book explores digital games as texts, as cultural industry and as cultural practice in contemporary European, American and some Asian societies. The book draws upon a range of theoretical perspectives and insights from media theory, especially political economy of the media, cultural studies, and sociology – in particular the sociology of science and technology.

One of the core perspectives applied in this book draws upon a critical political economy of the media approach. This approach is quite distinct from standard economics. Whereas standard economics is concerned with improving efficiency, competitiveness and profit, political economy is concerned with issues of power and inequality which operate in and through the media industries and media texts. There are different schools within the political economy approach, as Hesmondhalgh (2002) and Mosco (1996) usefully outline. In this book the approach has more in common with the continental tradition, which is concerned with relating the changing structure of the media industries, for example concentration and integration, with labour and textual issues. It is also concerned with how institutions and structures relate to individuals and their actions, which is a traditional concern of social theory more generally.

Political economists of the media have traditionally paid less attention to audiences and media use, except in terms of how they are constructed and sold to advertisers. This has meant that their work has been strongly critiqued from within cultural studies and perhaps much of this critique is best articulated by John Fiske (1987, 1992) in a number of publications. Clearly this is a major weakness and it is particularly so in relation to a cultural form that requires player input to create the textual experience in the first place, and which in many instances invites the player to adapt the original text. These formal changes must be considered in addition to our understanding of the polysemic nature and interpretation of texts. At the same time, user freedom is not unlimited, and political economic theories highlight how the media industries attempt to structure audiences according to demographics, contexts of use and cultures.

The arguments put forward by cultural theorists, particularly in relation to the extent to which audiences negotiate media texts, have in part been acknowledged by political economists. Garnham (2000), for example, includes a chapter on 'Audiences: interpretation and consumption'. At the same time he outlines what he sees as the limitations of cultural studies and audience research in terms of the false distinction between passive and active audiences and the dangers of confusing activity, or interactivity, with critical engagement. These points are well taken. Less useful is his rejection of pleasure as something that is opposed to rationality. While pleasure is a complex concept and means different things in different disciplines, it would seem foolish to reject pleasure a priori (Kerr et al., in press). Digital games in the main are entertainment products and pleasure, in all its complexity, is an essential goal of the production and consumption process.

A useful bridge between these two perspectives is provided by sociologists of science and technology (STS), who study how new technologies more generally, not just media technologies, are shaped by human actions within the wider context of existing social, cultural, political and economic factors. Technology in this literature is defined broadly to include the underlying technology, the content and the techniques needed to use them. If we apply this perspective to the development of a digital game, we can see the production process as a negotiated process in which humans and the technology play a role, but which cannot be understood without also examining the wider social, cultural, economic and political context. Indeed, while the process of making a digital game involves a team of people struggling to exploit the potential of particular technologies, it is interesting to observe the variations in this process from company to company and country to country.

STS researchers point to the implicit and explicit involvement of the user in all stages of the technological innovation process and thus overcome the distinction often made in media studies between production and consumption of media (Akrich and Latour 1992; Akrich 1995; Mackenzie and Wajcman 1999; Lievrouw and Livingstone 2002; Sørensen 2002). This work investigates the role that users play both in the initial design process and, after launch, in the continual improvement of that design over time.

Many STS studies have found that end users may develop new uses for a product or service which were unanticipated by the designers. They have also found that end users are an important source of information for future innovations. As a result, companies may employ very explicit techniques, such as user testing and market surveys, to gather information. However, the work of Madeleine Akrich (1992, 1995) also alerts us to the ways in which implicit assumptions about the user may be incorporated into the design of a product or service. She found that many designers base assumptions about users on their own tastes and interests, a process which she calls the 'I-Methodology'. Other scholars have explored the I-Methodology with regard to ICTs and have found examples of designers who, either consciously or unconsciously, inscribe certain biases and proscribe certain behaviours in their products (Oudshoorn and Pinch 2003; Oudshoorn et al. 2004). This perspective can help us to understand how both explicit market data and implicit assumptions about users shape the production and publishing of digital games (Kerr 2002).

Essentially this book attempts to explore the entire production cycle from producer to distributor to final user and the linkages and relationships between these stages. A number of recent books have attempted to visualise the relationship between media producers and media consumers in terms of circuits. Du Gay et al. (1997: 3) propose a circuit of culture model, which identified five major interconnected cultural processes including representation, identity, production, consumption and regulation. More recently Kline et al. (2003: 51) developed the Marxian production/commodity/consumption cycle to include technology, culture and marketing subcircuits. While these models are useful in terms of overcoming more linear models, and serve a pedagogic purpose, they are problematic in terms of drawing distinctions between processes that overlap and mutually shape one another. One must always be careful to acknowledge that such models may act to simplify complex social processes and divert attention away from other factors, peculiar to certain places and times. Others question the degree to which we can identify and talk about production and consumption as separate processes at all. Recent work from Marshall suggests that we need to study 'the way in which the populace is engaged in that process of cultural production' (Marshall 2004: 11). Similarly, Henry Jenkins writes about 'participatory culture' and 'interactive audiences' (2002: 157–70).

These difficulties may point to a wider social challenge, namely the blurring of boundaries between work and play in post-industrial, post-modern societies. This book analyses the very 'real' work which goes into the production of digital games around the world and the technologies on which they are played. The work culture in many development companies taps into the, by now familiar, characteristics of the culture industries: informal, relaxed, non-hierarchical, project based and contractual. Lunch time and coffee breaks are spent playing games and browsing work-related websites on the very computers used to make games. Weekends are used either to play games or to finish making games, depending on when the next deadline falls.

Playing digital games also resembles work. Notwithstanding the existence of professional game players, amateur game players put a lot of 'work' into playing and 'modding', or modifying, digital games; into levelling up, learning the codes and conventions, finding cheats, practising, participating in online communities, beta testing games, developing new characters or maps. Digital games, particularly the more complex ones, are challenging both to make and to play. The first digital games were developed during work, or downtime in work, by scientists working in publicly funded laboratories. They were playful diversions from real work and the inventors never thought that others might be employed some day to make such things. People who work in the industry are usually avid game players and often entered the industry because of their love for digital games. Cubitt (2001: 133) argues that in the age of simulation, 'we can no longer distinguish between play and work'. It would appear that distinguishing between production and consumption and between work and play in contemporary Western societies is increasingly problematic.

This book contributes to our understanding of this theoretical problematic and attempts to map some of its contours. While acknowledging that the digital game industries construct their market through the forms and types of games they produce and the marketing of them, the book also points to opportunities and attempts by game players to renegotiate, appropriate, bracket and reproduce those texts and marketing for their own purposes. The theoretical problematic maps onto a very real struggle for creative control on both sides, which is currently being played out in international trade and legal fora and in less obvious ways in homes and apartments around the world.

STRUCTURE OF THE BOOK

This book draws upon an extensive literature review and empirical research project conducted as part of a Government of Ireland and Dublin City University funded post-doctoral fellowship. The original project plan set out to explore three related dimensions of digital games – digital games themselves; the digital games industry; and digital game play/use – and to reflect on the implications for media and social theory. While the book roughly follows the original research plan, the content of the chapters differs from a conventional media text book in a number of ways.

First, many of the terms and theories are contested and there are few academics whose work has been accepted throughout the field. Second, there is a dearth of empirical work of any scale or which provides a longitudinal perspective either on the industry or on digital game play. Third, many of the books are written from an Anglo-American perspective; perspectives from other parts of the world remain to be written or translated. Finally, there is little agreement in this field as to the best methods to be used to study digital games. Despite these difficulties, this book is designed to give the student an overview of the key theories and research currently available in the English language.

Chapter 2 traces the origins of digital games and presents an overview of the contingent nature of their development. It goes on to examine digital games as text, a term which is increasingly problematic when applied to new media in general, and digital games in particular.

The chapter presents a review of the key theories used to understand digital games and a summary of the debate between those who use narrative theories to examine digital games, namely the *narratologists*, and those who reject that approach and look to play and game theory for inspiration, namely the *ludologists*.

Chapter 3 explores the characteristics and strategies that define digital games as a cultural industry and attempts to assess its economic value and growth in relation to more established media industries. The chapter goes on to examine the digital games industry value chain, the ownership structure and the power struggles between the various actors in this value chain. It also differentiates between four different sub-sectors or segments, namely: console games, standard PC games, massively multiplayer online games (MMOGs) and mini games.

Chapter 4 examines the cultures and processes of production in the PC and the console sub-sectors of the industry. It focuses on the global distribution and organisation of production and the gendered structure of the industry and working cultures in digital games companies in different parts of the world. The emphasis here is on understanding the production cycle from the development company's perspective and on the internal and external challenges they face – particularly in relation to publishers, technological change and users. It also explores the implicit and explicit role that users play in the game design process.

Chapter 5 examines matters of the audience and what happens after the retail stage of the production cycle. Again the term 'audience' is problematic when applied in the context of new media, and in this chapter it is replaced with the terms 'user' and 'player'. This chapter examines the data which are currently available on digital game players, on player pleasures, play preferences, play styles and play contexts. It presents an overview of large-scale surveys in a number of countries and then examines small-scale participant observation, interview and focus group studies. All of these point to the methodological and theoretical difficulties faced by researchers and the industry in terms of researching and understanding digital game play in practice.

Chapter 6 explores the use of digital games in non-entertainment contexts, focusing on education, learning and training in formal and informal contexts such as schools, universities, industry and the military. This chapter presents a range of work that argues that digital games can be usefully employed within education and training. It also highlights more sceptical arguments from those who are less than convinced and who point in particular to the gendered patterns of use which we risk exacerbating. It also presents a brief overview of government policies to promote media literacy and culture and explores the implications these may have for our understanding of digital games.

The concluding chapter summarises the key findings, relates them to our understanding of media texts, producers and audiences, and reflects on their implications for our understanding of the role of the media in society more generally.

TWO

DIGITAL GAMES AS TEXT

OVERVIEW

Digital games can be seen as a new application of a range of technological, social and economic inventions, some of which date back to
the late 1800s. This chapter starts by examining the origin stories
recounted by current game histories and explores why digital games
emerged in those particular places and times. This section highlights the
highly contingent, historically and culturally situated nature of digital
game developments.

The chapter then moves on to examine digital games as texts. The
reader is first introduced to the fact that the text, in terms of digital
games, is contested and problematic for game scholars. The reader is
then presented with different theoretical approaches to digital games.
Initially game scholars polarised into those who viewed digital games
as a new form of narrative – *the narratologists* – and those who opposed
this approach and viewed digital games first and foremost as games –
the *ludologists*. By 2004 something of an *entente* had emerged between
these two camps, with some academics trying to accommodate both
perspectives and others looking elsewhere for inspiration. The chapter
finishes with a short examination of genre and digital games.

A BRIEF HISTORY OF DIGITAL GAMES

The book *When Old Technologies Were New: Thinking about
Electric Communication in the Late Nineteenth Century* by Carolyn

Marvin (1988) is an exploration of electric media and the fascination and fear that people had for them in the late nineteenth century. Its focus is not on artefacts and inventors, but rather on the struggle between various interest groups to define a place for electric media in society.

Media historians argue that new technologies both shape and are shaped by social processes; moreover that the complexity of this interaction means that the results are unpredictable (Flichy 1995; Winston 1996, 1998). This is similar to an approach in sociology called 'social shaping', which argues that the diffusion of science and technology inventions from laboratory to market is neither inevitable nor unproblematic; rather the process involves a continuous struggle between different technological solutions, different constructions and different interest groups (Williams 1997; Mackenzie and Wajcman 1999; Lievrouw and Livingstone 2002). Indeed, the user plays an important part in this process and may develop uses for innovations which their designers never envisaged. A social shaping perspective on socio-technical change informs this brief history of digital games.

When one reads many contemporary histories of digital games, one is struck by the fact that they emphasise names and dates and play down controversy. J. C. Herz (1997: 13–31) divides her 'natural history' of games into 'eras', as any natural history museum might do. Poole (2000) extends the metaphor still further, opening his book with an invocation of the Genesis story followed by a chapter called 'The Origin of Species'. These histories are useful to the extent that they organise and classify messy social events into neat temporal boxes. However, they tell us little of the context from which the early digital games emerged or of the different paths that digital games took in different countries.

Both the aforementioned authors are fascinated with dates and naming inventors. Poole at least acknowledges that identifying dates and inventors is not an easy task, but asserts that Herz was 'erroneous' when she dated the first video game to the invention of *Spacewar* by Steven Russell at the Massachusetts Institute of Technology (MIT) in the USA in 1962. Poole (2000: 29) argues that, in fact, William Higginbotham developed the first video game four years earlier, as something to entertain visitors to the Brookhaven nuclear research facility in which he worked. However, he did not publicise or patent his invention. This debate raises the question: can someone be credited with inventing a new cultural form if they do not publicise it?

Our decision to use the term 'digital games' in this book takes on some significance as we examine these two origin stories – that of Higginbotham's *Tennis for Two* and Steven Russell's *Spacewar*. Higginbotham's game was presented on an 'analogue computer', a rather complicated network of amplifiers, vacuum tubes and transistors connected to an oscilloscope. Strictly speaking, this was not therefore a 'digital' game but one could argue it was a 'video' game. Steven Russell's *Spacewar* meanwhile was developed on a Digital Equipment Company (DEC) PDP-1, a large mainframe computer, and is described by Stephen Kent as the first 'interactive computer game' (Wolf 2001: 34–48). Wolf in the same book gives us an insight into the technical complexities of defining exactly what one means when one talks about a 'video' game. Consequently, the date one ascribes to the first digital game will be influenced by how one defines a digital game.

INVENTION CONTEXT

In order to understand why the first games were developed in these public research labs we must situate our dates, places and people in their wider historical context. Digital games on home consoles, in arcades or on PCs would not have been possible without the prior invention of a wide range of technological components from transistors (1947) to the cathode ray tube (1932) and integrated circuits (mid 1960s). Indeed, it is clear that the technological components to build the first digital games existed for some time before anyone actually put them together and developed one. Even when the first digital games were developed, it was not immediately obvious that they would become a commercial business. As media histories demonstrate, new practices do not emerge fully formed from a new technology, rather it is a creative process of negotiation between what Winston (1998) calls 'brakes' and 'accelerators' in particular cultural, economic and political contexts.

Digital games emerged in the USA during a time of complex socio-economic and geo-political changes. Globally it was the time of rock and roll music, the Space Race and the Cold War. Statistics show that by the late 1960s, in the USA in particular, employment levels in the agricultural and manufacturing industries were falling, while there was sustained growth in service industries, both public/government services and private services. The growth in public/government services was fuelled in part by the larger geo-political context of the time, but within this expansion one finds the establishment of the public research laboratories in which the first digital games were developed.

These structural shifts in employment led to major shifts in modes of living for many people. One of these shifts involved the move to 'self-servicing' domestic work, transport and entertainment (Miles and Gershuny 1983). Raymond Williams, writing in the early 1970s, described this period as the era of 'mobile privatisation' (Williams 1974: 26). A different Williams (2003) points to the increasing number of women entering the workforce, which exerted new time pressures on families and created a demand for domestic time-saving appliances. Kline et al. (2003: 84) describe the period as one of 'nuclear angst and consumer confidence', of 'drive-in cinemas', 'science-fiction films' and 'rocket fins'.

Two publications, emanating from different sides of the Atlantic, stand out for their attempt to establish why digital games emerged in the USA when they did, and how this invention context shaped the subsequent innovation trajectory. Haddon (1988, 1993) traces the links between the university computing departments, the military, the interests of the first game developers, the first games and the subsequent development of game playing as an activity embraced largely by young males. Haddon's work also explores how specific factors shaped the digital games market and industry in the UK.

The work by Kline et al. is in a similar vein and highlights 'the important role of cultural contexts and sub-cultural practices in the dynamics of innovation and design' (2003: 88). Like Haddon, the authors note the influence of publicly funded military-space research in the USA and the playful culture of the initial hackers/programmers on the development of the first games. They also point to the industry's origins in a highly masculine world and argue that this shaped the subsequent development of game genres, public game spaces and digital games as a cultural activity.

It is interesting to observe that the first games emerged, almost simultaneously, from two publicly funded science research institutes. Haddon (1993) notes that the first games were created by a group of people who were driven more by the 'intrinsic pleasure of experimenting' than by the search for profit. Darley (2000) and Kline et al.

(2003: 86) also focus on the 'playful' programming of the researchers/ programmers in the publicly funded research groups at this time. They also point to the influence of the wider media context on the types of games that these researchers invented. Darley argues that *Spacewar* was 'firmly rooted in the form and content of popular genres of the time – science fiction, Tolkienesque-fantasy and pinball' (2000: 25). It was far from obvious to Higginbotham and Russell that these playful 'hacks' would lead to the development of today's commercial games industry and culture.

FROM INVENTION TO INNOVATION

According to current histories, the first commercial digital games were launched almost simultaneously on two different platforms – the Baer/ Magnavox Odyssey console and its tennis and hockey games and Nolan Bushnell's/Atari coin-operated arcade game *Pong* (Poole, 2000: 32–3). 'Almost' is an important qualifier in the last sentence, because Magnavox went on successfully to sue Atari, and Atari ended up paying Magnavox a licence fee on every *Pong* game.

The background detail here points to a process of innovation based on trial and error. Nolan Bushnell grew up playing the freely available *Spacewar* as an engineering student in university. His first foray into the digital games field involved a collaboration with Nutting Associates, a pinball manufacturer, to produce the coin-operated arcade game *Computer Space* in 1971. This collaboration was unsuccessful but Bushnell learnt from the experience and went on to produce a much simpler coin-op game, *Pong*, with a more user-friendly interface. Ralph Baer meanwhile was working for a military electronics firm, Sanders Associates. By 1967 he had produced some rudimentary sports games and was looking for a business partner to exploit his ideas. He patented his 'TV gaming and training apparatus' in 1971 and in 1972 his design appeared as the Magnavox Odyssey, in association with Magnavox, a home electronics firm. What is interesting in these stories is that these two attempts to commercialise digital games happened almost simultaneously, on opposite sides of the USA, using different platforms and aimed at different markets; one at users in public spaces and the other at users in the home. Intriguingly, both ended up developing simple sports games.

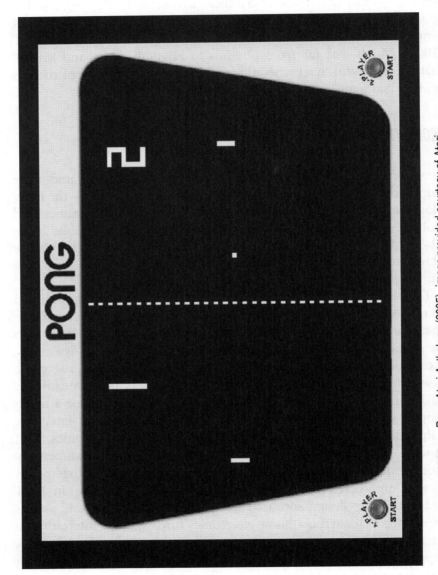

IMAGE 1 *Pong*, Atari Anthology (2005), image provided courtesy of Atari.

THE ATARI STORY

Bushnell formed Atari in 1972 and the undulating fortunes of Atari in different market segments provide us with a useful insight into the development of the wider digital games industry. Atari was so successful in the 1970s that it is said to have controlled up to 80 percent of the American market. It was bought by Warner Communications in 1976 for $28 million and was a very successful enterprise for Warner until a combination of bad product, aging consoles and poor management led to a drastic fall in profits and sales by the early 1980s. Poole (2000: 85) notes that Atari lost a considerable amount of money on an *ET* game in 1983, many of which were unsold and were dumped in a landfill site in New Mexico.

Atari's misfortunes continued and the company was unsuccessful with the Jaguar console in the early 1990s. It subsequently decided to focus its business solely on software. Between 1996 and 2000 Atari was sold three times, eventually being bought by a leading independent French publisher, Infogrames, who in 2003 changed their name to Atari.

Atari's history reflects the undulating growth of the games industry. It points to the increasing globalisation of the industry and ongoing, but not necessarily successful, industrial and content convergence with other media industries. One can see in Atari's history the difficulties faced by companies operating as a console manufacturer and there are interesting links between Atari and non-entertainment sectors like the army.

See www.corporate.infogrames.com/corp_history.php and the official Atari Historical Society website www.atarimuseum.com/mainmenu/mainmenu.html.

The decline of Atari in the late 1970s/early 1980s in the USA opened the door for other companies to enter the market. Herz (1997) notes that both Nintendo and Sega began exporting arcade games to the USA in 1981 and five years later the Nintendo Entertainment System (NES) and Sega's Master System – two console systems aimed at the home – were launched. In Herz's account two terse statements signal the entry of these two major Japanese companies into the North American market. Poole is somewhat more poetic:

> The big players in the late 1980s and [early] 1990s were two Japanese giants: Nintendo, with its NES and the more powerful Super NES; and Sega, with its Megadrive … Nintendo and Sega inspired fanatical

loyalty. They were the Beatles and Stones of the late 1980s and early 1990s. Nintendo was the Beatles; wholesome fun for all the family... Sega, on the other hand, were the snarling, street-smart gang, roughing it up for the hardcore videogame fans. (Poole 2000: 18)

It is hardly surprising that Nintendo and Sega saw a market opportunity in the USA just as Atari seemed to falter. However, neither Poole, Herz nor Kline reveals anything about the history of these two Japanese companies prior to their entry into the American market. Sheff (1993) gives us a better insight and notes the history of game playing in Japan and the origins of Nintendo as a playing card company in the nineteenth century. Aoyama and Izushi (2003) note that the success of microelectronics, manga and animated films in Japan provided an important foundation for Japan's digital games industry as well as important social legitimation.

Wark provides an interesting comparison between Atari and the Japanese games companies. He argues that Atari neglected the development of its games platform in favour of becoming a manufacturer of cheap computers:

> The company's games went from being hot product in 1980 to landfill in New Mexico. The Japanese-based firms, on the other hand, don't see anything demeaning in being a successful and innovative games company, developing interactive graphic media, rather than being a second rate computer company. (Wark 1994: 21)

If one were to focus on the console segment of the games industry, then one would move now to detail the entry of Sony and more latterly Microsoft into the digital games industry. However, this would ignore other histories, platforms, events and players. Kline et al. (2003: 90) and Haddon (1993: 126) look at the distinct but related trajectories of the arcades, the console and the personal computer. Haddon (1993) and later Cornford et al. (2000) argue that the promotion and availability of cheap personal computers (for example, the Sinclair, Acorn and the Commodore) in the UK in the 1980s strongly influenced the growth of the PC games market and wider development industry there. As with Atari, Haddon found that not all PC companies in the UK were keen to promote the 'gameness' of their machines and some preferred to focus on their multi-functionality, fearing that games constituted too limited and trivial a market.

These early struggles and uncertainties over how to situate and market the PC are mirrored by more contemporary attempts by Sony to broaden the market in the 1990s by promoting their PlayStation 2 as an 'entertainment system' rather than just a gaming system (Kerr 2003). A unique selling point for the GameCube, by comparison, is its non-hybrid, game-specific focus (Finn 2001). Certainly the last 30 years has seen an ongoing struggle to redefine the television as a non-broadcast performance space and the PC as a non-work entertainment space.

Another insight into the struggle to define and situate digital games in society over the past 30 years is provided by reviewing the main-stream press. When Williams (2002) examined the coverage of digital games by three major American news magazines from 1970–2000, he found that it mirrored the major periods of growth and decline of the industry – an increase between 1980 and 1982, a rapid decline in 1983 and again in 1991 and 1995, then steady growth until 2000. By 2000 he suggests that games were receiving as much coverage, in quantity terms, as film.

Williams also found a high frequency of articles framed in negative terms and that gender, health and violence were frequent themes. He notes that there was a 'consistent pattern of male technocratic privilege' in many of the articles and much attention was given to the displace-ment of healthy activities by games, the health risks of playing games, and the effects of game content on values, attitudes and behaviour – the latter specifically related to *Mortal Kombat* and the 1999 Columbine High School shootings. Williams also found a number of positive arti-cles about games, including those that argued that digital games pro-vide a safe/alternative playing environment.

In terms of explaining the negative frames in many of these stories, Williams points to the wider American context and rise of the con-servative Reagan administration. Historians of the media would argue that moral panics about new media are nothing new, as most new technologies challenge existing norms and threaten to disrupt established practices (Haddon 1993). Marshall argues that while computers are associated with work and education, videogames are seen as a waste of time and a waste of human resources (Marshall 1997; Morris and Marshall 2000). This attitude may be changing, as digital games are increasingly seen as a route into the computer industry. Further, these attitudes may be truer of the USA and cer-tain countries in Europe than Asia, where there appears to be a more positive attitude to gaming culture. Nevertheless, digital games have certainly inherited some of the negative connotations associated with amusements and popular entertainment.

A good social history of digital games remains to be written. Such a history would focus less on dates and inventors and more on struggles and uncertainties. Kline et al. ask: 'what if computer research had been funded not by the Pentagon but by educational or medical institutions?' (2003: 108). Indeed, what if the Brookhaven nuclear facility had patented their tennis game or if Nintendo had never approached Sony for assistance in developing a CD-ROM-based storage device – a move which indirectly led to Sony entering the games industry (Sheff 1993).

It is clear from this brief review of digital game histories that the story involves much more than technologies, inventors, dates and economics and that wider cultural and social contexts have played an important role. The broader context in which the first inventors developed their hacks and the first innovators developed the first commercial games influenced the choice of platform, partners and content developed. The wider context also meant that while in the USA and the UK digital games were often seen as harmful and trivial entertainment, in Japan the widespread success of manga, animation and other forms of game playing offered a degree of social legitimation.

DIGITAL GAMES AS MEDIA TEXT

Traditionally, in media studies the term media 'text' was used either to signal a narrow focus on the conventions and physical form of a media message – the film or the television programme – or to signal a broader focus on the physical form of the message combined with the meanings, as interpreted by the user/audience. Fiske, in particular, argues that a programme is produced by the media industry while a text is produced by its audience (1987: 14). The variability of digital games seems to challenge the narrow approach and points to a multiplicity of possible meanings and experiences at the level of the physical form of the message. This, in turn, may force us to assess whether traditional research methods, for example content analysis, are adequate for the task of examining digital games as texts.

Espen Aarseth (1997) argues that we need to extend the concept of the 'text' when it is applied to 'interactive texts' to include not only 'the mechanical organization of the text' and the role of the audience/user, but also the medium. He argues that one's experience of, for example, an adventure game, is influenced as much by the randomness built into the medium, as the choices made by the user and the organisation of the surface elements by the designer. Similarly, Ryan (1999: 97) argues that while a traditional text consists of two levels (*viz.* the text as a collection of signs written by the author and the text as constructed mentally by the reader), new media texts have three levels: the text as engineered by the designer/author; the text as presented to the reader; and the text as constructed mentally by the reader. While most scholars acknowledge the role of the medium in structuring a media text, digital media and digital game scholars in particular, are exercised by the changing user/text/medium relationship and the instability of the digital game text (see also Lister et al. 2002).

In what follows we shall explore some of the different theoretical approaches that have been used by game theorists to analyse digital games as media texts. This is a burgeoning literature and in the space provided we can only focus on key theories and theorists. In the main these theories are imported from other fields, although there is a strong sense that new terminology will be, and is being, invented as game studies gains recognition and popularity.

NARRATIVE THEORIES AND DIGITAL GAMES

In his later work Barthes showed that anything from a boxing match to a magazine advertisement could be viewed as a 'text' and its structure and meanings critically decoded (1970, 1977). His work opened the way for literary and media theorists to extend their work into new areas, including text-based computer games (see Aarseth 1997: 107–11 for example) and later three-dimensional (3D) digital games. Within literary and media studies, narrative theories are a key analytical tool. It is therefore perhaps unsurprising that practitioners from these disciplines should adopt and adapt these theories to the study of digital games.

The usefulness of both narrative and dramatic theories to the study of digital games is widely debated. Indeed, the history of these debates is well documented in the online archives of international conferences such as Computational Semiotics for Games and New Media (COSIGN) and the Digital Arts Conference (DAC),[1] on personal and individually run game websites,[2] and more latterly in the online journal *Game*

Studies.[3] While narrative theory is just one approach within literary theory, it has attracted by far the greatest attention within this debate (Frasca 1999; Juul 1999; Kücklich 2001, 2003; Ryan 2001). When the online journal *Game Studies* was launched, the first set of articles could be divided into those that viewed narrative theory as a fruitful approach to the study of digital games and those that rejected this approach. The first editorial stated:

> [M]uch of the industry and ... academic commentators see the need for 'narrative' structures in order to understand games and make games 'better'. In this issue, the debate about narratives' and narratology's relevance to game studies is clearly visible. This is a debate that shows the very early stage we are still in, where the struggle of controlling and shaping the theoretical paradigms has just started. (*Game Studies*, vol. 1, issue 1, July 2001)

Before we examine approaches in game studies to narrative, it might be useful to explore what the term 'narrative' means. In everyday usage 'narrative' and 'story' are often used interchangeably but in academia the terms have specific, if contested, definitions. The most common approach traces its roots back to Aristotle and his analysis of the core elements that underpin narrative in literary forms – characters, action, plot. For Aristotle, narrative has a beginning, middle and end, which are sometimes called the crisis, the climax and the resolution respectively. He also identified the strict causal and temporal relationship between events in a plot. Following on from this, it is suggested that narrative transcends media and therefore one can translate, or transpose, a narrative from one media to another. While media may have a configurative effect on a narrative, a certain conceptual core will be maintained (Lacey 2000; Ryan 2001; Nelmes 2003).

In media and literary studies, scholars generally differentiate between two parts of the narrative process: the story and the telling of the story. Thus, it is suggested that the story of a book can be separated from its telling, or the story of a film can be separated from its presentation in the film. The story and the way it is told in a film are referred to, respectively, as the 'fabula' and the 'syuzhet'. In film what is referred to as the 'classic' narrative structure had emerged by the 1930s and drew heavily on the literary approach to narrative. There are alternative narrative structures, including avant-garde and counter-cinema (for example, *Last Year at Marienbad* (1961), *Pulp Fiction* (1994), *Run Lola Run* (1998) and *Time-Code* (2000)) but the classic narrative structure still dominates (Cook 1985). This structure has led to the development of certain film-specific narrative conventions with regard to editing, point-of-view and characterisation. While Seymour Chatman uses slightly different terms, his definition of narrative is useful:

> [E]ach narrative has two parts: a story (histoire), the content or chain of events (actions, happenings), plus what may be called the existents (characters, items of setting); and a discourse (discours), that is, the expression, the means by which the content is communicated. In simple terms, the story is the What in a narrative ... discourse [is] the How. (1978: 19)

The classical approach to narrative is very much a product of the modernist era and post-structuralist theorists question some of its premises, including the supposed causality between events and the role given to the reader/user in the process. An example of the post-structuralist approach to narrative is provided by Marsha Kinder, who is a proponent of a more discursive and culturally specific approach, and this allows her to 'see games as a special kind of narrative' (2002: 122). Kinder is more interested in the cognitive and ideological function of narrative than its structure.

Marie-Laurie Ryan (2001) also adopts a post-structuralist approach to narrative and suggests that new interactive literary forms demand that we rethink our understanding of narrative. She contends that there can be different types of narrative: *conventional dramatic narratives*, where a semantic structure accords with the Aristotelian principles; *sequential narratives*, where events are ordered in a temporal sequence; and *causal narratives*, where an interpretation of events invokes causality (2001: 242–6). New media and digital games are forcing both literary theorists and media theorists to rethink what is meant by narrative. For as Silverstone (1999: 44) posits, 'while it is perfectly acceptable to see in contemporary narratives echoes of earlier forms ... it would be a mistake to insist that such perspectives exhausted the complexities of our own media culture.'

In the 1990s a body of work emerged from within post-structuralist literary theory which viewed digital games as a new form of 'interactive text' which challenged the narrow, formal approach to understanding and analysing narrative and positioned the user as a central player in the process (Turkle 1984; Laurel 1993; Landow 1997; Murray 1997; Ryan 1999). Janet Murray (1997) provides us with an insight into this approach. She sees digital technologies as providing the potential for new forms of narrative and storytelling to emerge. Murray identifies digital games as one new type of 'story-telling format' (1997: 28) or 'narrative art', and in digital media she sees a loosening of boundaries between stories and games (1997: 64). While she emphasises that one cannot use old standards to judge these new formats (1997: 28), she nevertheless goes on to state that current digital games have very 'thin' narrative content, much of which is imported from other media. She believes that they have 'potential for more' and for the creation of 'new dramatic experiences' – a claim which is hotly contested by the ludologists and to which we shall return later in the chapter. For Murray 'games are always stories', but she acknowledges there is a need for a new term to capture the agency that digital games afford the player. She goes on to call them 'cyber-dramas'.

Another example of this work is provided by Brenda Laurel, who argued that the computer should be perceived as a medium and not as a tool. For her the computer creates opportunities 'for creative, interactive experiences, and ... for new forms of drama' (Laurel 1993: xi). She argues that computer games move interface design on from manipulation to engagement and participation. Drawing upon Aristotelian poetics and drama theories, Laurel seems to rate their narrative potential more highly than Murray, saying that they 'incorporate notions about character and action, suspense and empathy and other aspects of dramatic representation' (1993: 52–3).

The adoption of post-structuralist approaches to narrative has not deterred some media theorists from using a classical approach to narrative – albeit with some awareness of its limitations. A recent contribution by Wolf (2001) applies terminology which would be familiar to media students, for example, diegesis, mise-en-scène, point-of-view. He traces the historical development of a number of narrative elements including character types, cut scenes, moving cameras and points-of-view. Wolf also points to what he calls 'extra diegetic' narration, meaning things that are outside of the game world, including manuals and packaging. While he acknowledges that games may compare unfavourably with 'the complex and detailed ones found in other media' (2001: 93), like Murray he insists that digital games have not yet realised their potential and that there are possibilities for new types of narrative construction.

IMAGE 2 *Tomb Raider* © Core Design Ltd. (2005), used with permission of Eidos Interactive Ltd.

Similarly, Atkins (2003) uses a classical approach to formally analyse four contemporary digital games including *Tomb Raider, Half-Life, Close Combat* and *SimCity*. Atkins argues that digital games can usefully be analysed as a form of narrative fiction just like films, television and novels. In his analysis of *Tomb Raider,* for example, he outlines the filmic narrative strategies used by the game, such as intertexts, use of cameras, cut-scenes for plot establishment and advancement and draws parallels to traditional quest narratives from early folk tales. He goes on to outline where digital games may deviate from traditional narrative structures, including the tension created by the possibility of death, the limited freedom of choice, the hidden sub-plots and the potential for subversive readings of the text.

We shall see in the next section that narrative theories have been strongly criticised as a hegemonic aesthetic framework which may limit our analytical and critical analysis of digital games. Nevertheless various versions of narrative theory have been applied by some scholars to digital games and usefully highlight the continuities and differences between old and new media (Carr et al. 2003). It is worth remembering when reading the literature that game theorists generally adopt one of three approaches to narrative: a narrow, formalist and classical approach; a broad, culturally and historically located, post-structuralist approach; or an outright rejection of narrative theories. Given both the diversity of narrative theories and the diversity of games, some of which are clearly more narrative driven than others, it would be unwise to dismiss narrative theory outright.

One of the problems with applying classical narrative theories to games is that one is transposing theories from static texts to more dynamic texts. Of course, this problem is not unique to digital game scholars. As radio and television move from analogue to digital and expand to introduce new interactive applications and services, the same challenges arise. As such, it is not unique to digital game studies that there is less emphasis on character and linear forms of narrative and more attention paid to non-linear narratives, environments, spectacle and interactivity (Cubitt 1998, 2001; Darley 2000).

A CRITIQUE OF NARRATIVE THEORIES AS APPLIED TO DIGITAL GAMES

One of the first scholars to publish on the limitations of narrative theories as applied to digital games was Ted Friedman. Friedman's (1995) conceptualisation of narrative goes beyond the classical approach but he also argues that there is a need for new theories to take account of the specificities of digital games. He provides a critique of core literary concepts like 'the reader' and 'the text' and he argues for the development of a 'software theory' or some form of alternative model in order to understand complex simulation games like *The Sims* (2000) and *Civilization II* (1996). For Friedman, computer games are marked by the potential for interaction between the player and the text that the underlying computer technology allows for – what he calls a 'cybernetic circuit.' Friedman notes that complex simulation games do not have characters and plot in the conventional narrative sense. Furthermore he shows that they differ from traditional film or print narratives in that one identifies with the overall process, or system, rather than particular characters in the game. For Friedman, the primary narrative agent in these games is 'geography' and he goes on to call these games 'spatial stories' or cognitive maps. What is interesting in Friedman's work is the suggestion that narrative theory may be inadequate to analyse complex simulation games.

Another literary scholar, Espen Aarseth, emerged around the same time as Friedman and similarly provided a critique of existing attempts to apply narrative approaches to digital games. Interestingly, Aarseth has become something of a standard-bearer for those game scholars who reject narrative theory as an approach to digital games, i.e. the ludologists. Before we examine play theories and the work of the ludologists, it is useful to explore Aarseth's early work which led to the development of a new focus on play and games in game studies and the narratology/ludology debate.

Intriguingly, Aarseth (1997) barely refers to play or game theorists and his initial argument refers primarily to text-based adventure games, although it has subsequently been applied more widely to digital games. Aarseth maintained that many early attempts to apply narrative theories to games fail to grasp the intrinsic qualities of digital games because they tend to privilege the 'aesthetic ideals of ... narrative literature' (1997: 106). He argues that: 'the most interesting feature of these texts is their difference from, and not their (inferior) resemblance to, the hegemonic forms. What makes them worthy of study is the fact that they present an alternative mode of discourse'. (1997: 109). Similar arguments have subsequently been developed by Frasca (1999, 2003) and Juul (1999, 2001).

Aarseth comes from a literary theory background and his approach to the analysis of interactive texts is highly formalist. In common with

Murray, Kinder and Laurel he sees the computer as having the potential to create new forms of literature, or texts, and he traces the characteristics which these new forms share with traditional literary texts (Aarseth 1997: 21). However, in contrast to Murray, Kinder and Laurel, he feels that narrative theory is too limiting and argues that we 'need to dispose of the poetics of narrative literature and use the computer's potential for combination and world simulation to develop new genres' (1997: 21). For Aarseth, digital games are part of a particular genre called 'cybertexts', which are distinguished by the fact that non-trivial effort is required from the user to work through them. Despite the name, cybertexts are not necessarily anything to do with computers. Examples of cybertexts range from the ritualistic *I Ching* (circa 1,000 BC) to poems like Apollinaire's *Calligrammes* (1916) and onto early games like *Adventure* (1976) and hypertext novels like *Afternoon* (1990).

Aarseth also critiques the traditional threesome of the author/sender, text/message and reader/receiver and talks instead, as Friedman (1995) does, of the 'cybernetic intercourse' between the operator/user, the verbal sign and the medium. In his analysis of the internal structure of the text-based game *Adventure,* this cybernetic intercourse is explicated. His model of this adventure game describes four groups of components: the data, the processing engines, the interface and the users. Information flows between all four components during play (1997: 104). For Aarseth the processing engines are the 'heart' of a game, deciding the course of the action based on a combination of user input, the state of the game world and the underlying game rules and how this should be represented to the user.

Aarseth argues that many of the core terms within classical narrative theory simply do not apply to textual adventure games and he rejects both classical and post-structuralist definitions of narrative. Indeed, he argues there may not be a story at all in digital games, merely a plot, or what he calls an 'intrigue', which the user must figure out (1997: 112). An intrigue is similar to Chatman's concept of story or the 'what' that is transmitted by the text. An intrigue contains events (actions and happenings) and existents (characters and settings) but Aarseth claims they are not connected in a fixed, causal sequence as in a classical or modernist narrative. For him a cybertext is a multidimensional event space which unfolds through the negotiation of the space by the user, who takes on the role of the main character. For Aarseth the dominant user function in adventure games is configurative, not interpretative as in classical narratives (1997: 62–5).

Aarseth's 1997 work is sometimes difficult to position in the narratology/ludology debate. His literary theory background and language are similar to many of the narratologists and in his 1997 book he does not refer to play and game theorists and only in one chapter does he focus on a game. But his critique of narrative theory and his approach to the analysis of cybertexts has proved inspirational to many and thus provides a useful segue into the work of the ludologists. Since 1997 Aarseth has continued to critique narrative theories while still being concerned with issues of story, character and time in digital games. He states in a later work that the 'traditional hermeneutic paradigms of text, narrative and semiotics are not well-suited to the problems of a simulational hermeneutic. Games (as games) might be the best empirical entry point to this new mode of discourse' (Aarseth 2004: 54).

PLAY THEORIES AND DIGITAL GAMES

While narratologists draw upon a pre-existing heritage of narrative theories and analysis of other media, ludologists also draw inspiration from a pre-existing heritage of work on non-digital play and games. In order to understand the work of the ludologists, we need to take a brief detour.

Defining what is a game and what is play is not a straightforward task. The *Oxford Reference Dictionary* (1987) defines the verb 'to play' as 'to occupy oneself in a game or other recreational activity, to act light-heartedly or flippantly, to compete … to move a piece in a game, to perform'. As a noun it means recreation, amusement, especially the spontaneous activity of children. One can also play around with, play at, play back, play the market. Meanwhile the same dictionary defines a game as 'a form of play or sport, especially a competitive one organised with rules, penalties, a portion of play forming a scoring unit, a series of contests, a scheme.' It goes on to explain the meaning of game theory – a branch of maths that deals with the best strategies for participants in conflict and which is widely applied in the economic and political sciences.

From these dictionary definitions we can start to define games as rule bound, goal orientated situations where there are clear winners and losers. However, some play situations can also display these characteristics. A recent book on game design argues that games can be seen as a subset of play in the broadest terms, but that play can also be seen as a component of games: '[P]lay and games have a surprisingly complex relationship. Play is both a larger and a smaller term than "game", depending on the way it is framed' (Salen and Zimmerman 2003: 72–3).

There are three key play theorists whose work is referenced widely by ludologists. The first is Johan Huizinga; a Dutch academic, whose book *Homo Ludens* (1949) asserts that play existed prior to culture and goes on to describe numerous types of play in society, from children's games to contests, theatrical representations and games of chance. Huizinga defines play as a 'voluntary activity or occupation executed within certain fixed limits of time and place, according to rules freely accepted but absolutely binding' (1949: 28). Key features for Huizinga are that play is outside ordinary life, is not associated with material interest or profit, is bounded in time and space, is rule bound, voluntary and creates social groups that separate themselves from the outside world.

For Huizinga, play takes place in areas that are clearly demarcated. His list of playgrounds includes the concept of the magic circle, which we will see later has been taken up by ludologists.

> All play moves and has its being within a play-ground marked off beforehand either materially or ideally, deliberately or as a matter of course ... the arena, the card-table, the magic-circle, the temple, the stage, the screen, the tennis court, the court of justice, etc., are all in form and function play-grounds, i.e. forbidden spots, isolated, hedged round, hallowed, within which special rules obtain. (Huizinga 1949: 10)

A second key play theorist whose work is widely quoted is Roger Caillois (2001). To some extent Caillois built upon Huizinga's work and he also defines play as free and separate in time and space. He notes that play and games can be distinguished by the fact that in the former rules are looser or non-existent. For Caillois games have six formal qualities: freedom, separateness (in time and space from events outside), rules, uncertainty of outcome, non-productiveness and make-believe (2001: 9–10). Another important contribution which digital game theorists have drawn upon is Caillois's continuum, which categorises games according to the degree of paidia (meaning improvisation) or ludus (meaning rule bound). For him, some games have clear winning states/goals and thus can be placed closer to the ludus end of a spectrum, while less goal-directed games can be placed closer to the paidia end of a spectrum. One could, for example, place *The Sims 2* (2004) towards the paidia end of the spectrum and *Prince of Persia: The Sands of Time* (2003) towards the ludus end of the spectrum.

Caillois also identified four different modes of play, some of which can co-exist in games: competition (agôn), chance (alea), simulation (mimicry) and vertigo (ilinx). Agôn exists in games where the conditions are set, so that opponents have an equal chance of winning but they can each influence the outcome, like in football and chess. Alea can be found in lotteries and roulette, where the winner is decided by fate and the throwing of a dice. Mimicry, or make-believe, exists when players make others believe that they are someone other than themselves, as in role-playing games. Finally, ilinx refers to the destruction of order and stability, as in merry-go-rounds where one can become dizzy.

The final major play theorist we will examine is Brian Sutton-Smith, who has written a number of key publications on play (Avedon and Sutton-Smith 1971). Juul (2001) provides a useful overview of his work in an article in *Game Studies*. Salen and Zimmerman (2003: 78) refer to Sutton-Smith as 'the most prolific and important scholar of play and games in the twentieth century'. A psychologist by training, his work draws upon theories and insights from many different disciplines and is empirically rich. In the 'Ambiguity of Play' (1997) Sutton-Smith points to one of the key methodological challenges facing play and game researchers: 'Because forms of play, like all other cultural forms, cannot be neutrally interpreted, it is impossible to keep ambiguity from creeping into the relationship between how they are perceived and how they are experienced' (1997: 216).

Sutton-Smith also asserts that play is diverse and goes on to identify nine different play forms: subjective play, solitary play, playful behaviours, informal social play, vicarious audience play, performance play, celebrations and festivals, contests (games and sports), risky or deep play. Of interest to students of digital games are the examples he gives of four of these forms: *solitary play*, which includes using computers and watching videos; *vicarious audience play*, which includes television, films and concerts; *informal social play*, which includes use of the internet; and *contests*, which include card and board games.

More recently, Salen and Zimmerman (2003) provide a useful overview of game theories from the perspective of game designers and note that the only consensus between game theories is that all games have rules. They define a game as 'a system in which players engage in an artificial conflict, defined by rules, that result in a quantifiable outcome' (2003: 80). They use Huizinga's concept of the 'magic circle' as a core concept to refer to 'the special place and time created by a game' (2003: 95) but they note that this place or circle is both closed and open at the same time. Thus, while games are clearly demarcated from reality and operate within rules, they are influenced by what players bring into them and do, and are situated within culture at large. As such, for these authors rules, play and culture are three interlinked dimensions from which to understand a game (2003: 101–5).

Looking beyond these play theorists, there have been some interesting contributions on play within the media and communications field. Marshall McLuhan wrote a chapter on games and their role in society just after Roger Caillois in 1964. McLuhan decribes games as voluntary activities, which have uncertain outcomes and operate according to strict conventions and rules. He goes on to define games as 'media of interpersonal communication [that] could have neither existence nor meaning except as extensions of our immediate inner lives' (1964: 253).

McLuhan is concerned with the role of games in society and argues that with the development of literary and more individualised societies, games and rituals changed from being models of cosmic dramas to models of 'inner psychological life'. At the same time, he sees games as extensions of social man, as a form of popular art and reflective of the wider and changing culture from which they stem. He also sees them as a popular response to 'workaday stress' (1964: 250). While McLuhan conflates the medium and the message in this chapter and does not seem to allow that there might be considerable variety between different types of game content (his focus is on sports, card games and quiz shows), his argument about the role of games in society reflects those of Huizinga, Caillois and Sutton-Smith.

More recently within media and communications, the concept of play has been used as a metaphor for the user's engagement with and use of new media generally. John Fiske (1987) asserts that play can be seen as a strategy of resistance which consumers can use to signal and assert their dissatisfaction with the capitalist structures of Western society. Roger Silverstone (1999: 59–67) argues that play is at the core of everyday life and can be used as a metaphor and tool for the analysis of media experiences. He compares play with electronic media to play in the carnivalesque society, although he notes that the boundaries between play and seriousness are less distinct and more permeable these days (1999: 62). Others, such as Marshall, have written about the rise of a 'play aesthetic' in the media: '[I]n the last decade of the twentieth century, the key insight to permeate the various culture industries, but particularly film and television, is that play is not limited to childhood or to sports' (Marshall 2002: 73).

THE LUDOLOGISTS, PLAY THEORIES AND DIGITAL GAMES

The work of Murray, Kinder and others who apply varying definitions of narrative and drama to games – a group who have been called the narratologists – is strongly criticised by a loose amalgam of critics often referred to as the ludologists (*ludus* means play in latin) (Aarseth 1997, 2004; Frasca 2003; Eskelinen 2004). These writers assert that there is a need for new theories and models to be developed if we are to understand what is unique about digital games as interactive texts. In the first instance they look to traditional play and game theories for inspiration – although they do not tend to refer to the work of media and communications scholars on play.

The ludologists emerged towards the end of the 1990s, to some extent as a counterbalance to the focus on narrative by other scholars. As already mentioned, Espen Aarseth proved inspirational to many by attempting to develop his own models of particular texts rather than import or adopt pre-existing models. For him games are not 'textual' or at least not primarily textual (2004: 47). He argues that theorists need to study the 'game-world-labyrinth' dimension of cybertexts (1997: 5) and more recently that 'any game consists of three aspects: (1) rules, (2) a material/semiotic system (a gameworld) and (3) gameplay (the events resulting from the application of the rules to the gameworld)' (2004: 47–8). For Aarseth the semiotic is not the most important. Similarly, Gonzalo Frasca draws upon Roger Caillois' concepts of paidia and ludus to argue that cybertexts and video games should be analysed as games (1999) and for a move away from representation towards simulation semiotics or '*simiotics*' (2003: 223). For Frasca, the fact that games simulate and model behaviours rather than represent them is key. Frasca runs a website on ludology and is widely credited with coining the term. Both Frasca and Aarseth warn against the threat of theoretical imperialism and the colonisation of game studies by theories from other fields.

In a recent edited collection, Markku Eskelinen (2004) states that despite the work of the three play theorists already mentioned, games are under-theorised. For Eskelinen two key aspects of digital games mark them as different from traditional narratives; (i) the time scheme/ causality of events and (ii) the nature and role of the character/user. He states that 'the dominant temporal relation is the one between user time and event time, and not the narrative one between story time and discourse time' (2004: 37). Eskelinen argues that characters in games are functional and a means to an end, what he calls combinatorial, and thus operate in a different way to characters in traditional narratives. For Eskelinen the user of a digital game is, to adopt Aarseth's term, ergodic and dynamic, as compared to the more static and interpretative role afforded to users of literature, film and drama.

Another key figure in this group is Jesper Juul. In his MA thesis, Juul (1999) argues that digital games are more game than story and therein lies their strength. For him the difficulties involved in translating a narrative from a film or novel into a game signal that narrative features are less important in digital games than gamelike features. In later work, Juul (2004) focuses on different elements in games, including time. Adopting a somewhat more macro perspective, Stuart Moulthrop (2004: 60) sees the 'shift from narrative to ludic engagement with texts and from interpretation to configuration' as symptomatic of wider shifts in society and in our relationship to information systems. Following Eskelinen, he notes that configuration, or the user's capacity to transform a virtual world, is not only an aspect of digital games but can also be applied to other new media like blogs, websites and e-mail.

Like narrative theories, non-digital play and game theories may also need adaptation to the world of digital games. Pervasive games, for example, challenge concepts like the 'magic circle', which is based on the notion that games are outside ordinary life. Indeed, it is clear that in many cases digital games are made, and sometimes played, for material gain and profit. Thus, while it is widely accepted by game scholars, not just the ludologists, that non-digital game and play theories are fundamental to an understanding of the digital games as texts, they are not without their problems and also require adaptation (Kücklich 2003).

Even as the ludologists were making their most stringent critique of narrative approaches to digital games, other scholars – not normally associated with game theories – were drawing upon the work of Huizinga, Caillois and Sutton-Smith. Provenzo (1991), for example, draws upon Johan Huizinga's concept of the 'playground' to describe Nintendo's products, although he was of the opinion that video games, as then constituted, provided a very limited play environment. Marsha Kinder (1991), in the same year, explored cognitive and psychological theories of play and how they relate to a child's development. Mark Wolf (2001) noted the importance of game elements like conflict, rules, player ability and outcome to digital games. Defining and identifying the ludologists is in itself problematic and even scholars like Janet Murray, usually associated with the narratologists, can utter statements more reminiscent of the ludological stance (Moulthrop 2004). Indeed, it is likely that the ludological term will be applied more broadly in the future to refer to the field of game studies rather than a small group within it.

OTHER THEORETICAL APPROACHES TO DIGITAL GAMES

In the last two sections we have seen how digital games challenge our understanding of, and theories about narrative, games and play. As digital games developed from relatively simple, text-based games into 3D and increasingly realistic graphical games, an increasing number of scholars have attempted to trace the influence of existing audiovisual traditions in television and film on digital games and, similarly, the influence of visual conventions in digital games on other audiovisual media (Bolter and Grusin 2000; Darley 2000; Poole 2000; Harries 2002; King and Krzywinska 2002b; Lister et al. 2002). For many of these scholars narrative is only one, usually minor, element of the complex multi-sensory game experience.

Bolter and Grusin (2000: 89–98) argue that digital games 'remediate' both television's hypermediated form and film's more immediate form. Poole (2000) points to the similarity between the use of replays in racing games and on television and the increasing links between digital games and film. He argues that digital games have influenced film styles, from *BladeRunner* to *The Matrix* and there is an increasing tendency to develop game–film tie-ins, for example, *Tomb Raider*. For Poole the use of full motion video sequences (FMV), or cut-scenes, which advance digital game plots and are watched instead of played, and the use of filmic camera angles in digital games illustrate the degree to which the two forms are interlinked. Nevertheless, he goes on to suggest that film and digital games could never merge without losing what is fundamental to each: that is to say, that one watches a film whereas one participates and controls an activity in digital games. Interestingly, the presumption that watching is something we do with films and television and controlling is something we do with games is increasingly problematised by studies of game players and play, an issue to which we shall return in Chapter 5 (Newman 2000a, 2000b).

In a similar vein, another book explicitly set out to examine the relationship between cinema and digital games (King and Krzywinska 2002b). In one chapter the relationship between narrative and spectacle in films and adventure games is compared. For King (2002), narrative is less prominent in games than in films, and while spectacle is an important way of selling a game, its contemplation is undermined by the need for interactivity within the game. Indeed, he argues that games may extend our understanding of the 'impact-aesthetic' (2002b: 61) whereby new interfaces like the dual-shock controller can translate the visual into a physical sensation. In another chapter, Mactavish explores the primacy of graphics, audio and gameplay in first-person shooter games and provides a critique of linguistics-based theories which, he argues, reduce the multi-sensory experience of digital media to language and tend to downplay the role of spectacle and special effects. For Mactavish, even in the most strongly narrative of today's computer games, narrative is only 'one element in a mixture contributing to gaming pleasure' (2002b: 38).

In another publication, Darley makes a similar argument when he states that digital games 'play up form, style, surface, artifice, spectacle and sensation, and they dilute meaning and encourage intellectual quiescence. They tend towards pure diversion, consisting of forms that are immediate and ephemeral in their effect' (Darley 2000: 6).

It is argued by media historians that over time, new media tend to develop unique forms (Williams 1974). Developing this theme, Darley (2000: 147) argues that digital games have developed new ways of soliciting engagement and participation from end users. King (2002: 54) makes a similar point when he refers to the various 'modes of engagement' which games make possible. With my colleagues I have explored the importance of control, immersion and performance as key dimensions of the digital game play experience (Kerr et al. 2006). In all these works it is clear that the user/ text/medium relationship is increasingly complex. Not only do we have complexity at the point of reception but we also have increasing complexity at the level of the text and the medium. Lev Manovich (2001: 245) sees digital games as an important site where the representational mode of traditional media texts meets the

IMAGE 3 *Halo 2* (2004) image provided courtesy of Microsoft.

control paradigm of computer science. For Mackenzie Wark, digital games represent:

> a significant step away from the intensity of cinema and the simultaneity of television ... Its aesthetic depth lies firstly in the complexity of possible interactions between the audience and the media text. Nintendo recognised this early. It developed the complexity of the vectors of interaction, not the quality of the graphics on the screen. (1994: 23)

Despite the relative youth of digital games there are some distinguishing characteristics of the form which mark it as unique and which have been underscored by those who have tried to extend our understanding of the 'text'. The player in a digital game is both the spectator and the protagonist. Apart from the cut scenes, the user is in control of the progress of the sequence and the game responds with varying degrees of sophistication to the user. The response mechanisms of digital games are increasingly sophisticated and multi-modal, involving audio, visuals and touch. The content and form of the game can be adapted using cheats or by hacking the underlying code. These developments pose a considerable theoretical and methodological challenge to those who wish to apply established theoretical perspectives to digital games – from narrative to play to representation. It is worth remembering, however, that digital games are diverse and that the ideas developed in relation to one game may not necessarily apply to other games, even in the same genre. Further, the rather under-theorised nature of game genres, the development of genre hybrids, and the emergence of new genres pose a constant challenge to game theorists.

DIGITAL GAME GENRES

One of the primary issues faced by game theorists, regardless of their theoretical approach, is the diversity of games. Grouping games together into genres, defined by some core characteristics, might be a solution to this problem. Currently, however, game genres are based more on poorly defined social conventions rather than clearly defined lists of characteristics. Nevertheless game genres arguably operate in the same way as film genres in that they act 'as systems of orientations, expectations and conventions that circulate between industry, text and subject' (Neale 1980).

Herz (1997) identifies eight different digital game genres, while Poole (2000) lists nine. The main differences between these two categorisations revolve around defining action, simulation and strategy games. For Herz, action games are a fairly broad church, while Poole distinguishes between shoot' em-ups, racing games and platform games. Poole admits that the term 'platform games' is probably outdated now and a more appropriate term might be 'exploration game' or adventure game (2000: 44). Meanwhile, Herz would categorise *SimCity* as a simulation game and *Civilization* as a strategy game, while Poole would call both 'god games'. Table 2.1 attempts to align the generic categories described by these two authors and outlines the defining features provided by them. It is clear that narrative and story are less important in the first four genres.

Genre is quite under-theorised in game studies but there have been some attempts to define what lies behind the generic categories. For Craig Lindley (2003) game genres can be distinguished depending on the balance of narrative, gameplay and simulation in a game. His taxonomy involves examining the balance between simulation, gameplay and narrative in a game and between fiction/non-fiction and virtuality/physicality. Using this taxonomy, he notes that role-playing games generally contain more narrative content than action games.

Many contemporary game titles are genre hybrids and new titles may defy classification, for example, rhythm/music games like *PaRappa The Rapper* (1996) and *Eye Toy* (2003). They may also vary from culture to culture. A recent survey in Japan identified 22 game genres, including the following: simulation RPG, action RPG, strategic simulation, nurturing/love simulation, rhythm-action, shooting, battle-type network games, RPG-type network game (CESA 2002: 77). Meanwhile ihobo, a group of game designers and scriptwriters, have defined 16 game genres including shooter, adventure, arcade adventure, bat and ball, fighting, sim, puzzle, racer, strategy and computer RPG, sports, rhythm dance, collector, platform, video pinball and video board game (see www.ihobo.com). What is striking about many genre lists is that there are often no categories for educational games, gambling and betting games.

Game genres also develop over time. For example, we have had shooters since the beginning of digital games. However, more recently a subgenre of shooters has developed called first-person shooter (FPS). *Wolfenstein 3D* (1992), *Doom* (1993), *Quake* (1996), *Half-Life* (1998). *Counter-Strike* (2000) and *Halo* (2001) took their lead (Bryce and

Table 2.1 A comparison of Herz and Poole's game genres

Herz (1997)	Poole (2000)	Defining Characteristics	Examples
Action	Shoot' em ups	Twitch First-person perspective Graphics Multiplayer mode Character and level modifications Missions	*Spacewar* *Half-Life* *Doom* *Quake* *Counter-Strike*
	Racing Games	Graphics Speed Power-ups Accurate simulations	*Gran Turismo* *Project Gotham Racing*
Fighting	Beat' em ups	Complex button combinations Motion capture Power-ups	*Tekken* *Mortal Kombat*
Sports	Sports	Combination of action and simulation Celebrity athletes Celebrity commentators Realism	*Pong* *NBA Inside Drive* *Tiger Woods Golf* *Pro Evolution Soccer* *Jonah Lomu rugby*
Puzzle	Puzzle	Exercises in logic Finding the right steps and the right order	*Tetris*
Adventure	Platform	Accumulate items Puzzles Power-ups Overcome obstacles Detailed back stories	*Legend of Zelda* *Tomb Raider* *Donkey Kong* *Prince of Persia* *Mario*
Role playing	Role playing	Statistics Maps Detailed back stories Focus on character Magic	*Ultima Online* *Legend of Zelda* *Ocarina of Time* *Shenmue*
Simulation	God games	Simulation of real-world environments and activities Realism	*Flight Simulator* *SimEarth* *Theme Hospital* *Roller Coaster Tycoon*
Strategy	Real time strategy games	Game play and goals generally abstract Often multiplayer Time element in RTSGs Logical thinking	*Civilization* *Age of Empires* *Command and Conquer*

Rutter 2002b; Järvinen 2002; Mactavish 2002). Another game design website notes that collector games led to the development of platform games and subsequently to adventure games (www.ihobo.com). Further, puzzles are increasingly incorporated into different game genres as a gameplay element. What is clear from this overview of existing generic analysis is that game genres are poorly defined and evolve as new technologies and fashions emerge.

> [E]ven video games, which, of all the forms at issue here, operate with perhaps the clearest sense of a generic classification … [are] somewhat crudely drawn relative to those in earlier/other popular cultural fields, but, already, description is becoming confused and problematic because of the rapidity with which earlier distinctions are blurring through hybridization. (Darley 2000: 142)

SUMMARY

Digital games are clearly shaped by a wide range of social and cultural factors, by non-digital games, social and cultural traditions of play and existing media forms. At the same time digital games are transmedial, hybrid and constantly evolving. Given the diversity of games and game platforms, all the theoretical perspectives examined above provide useful insights and help us to understand digital games as text and their relationship to the wider media and social environment. They also help us to address societal concerns about the role of digital games in society and the effects of their content.

NOTES

1 See *www.cosignconference.org/* and *http://hypertext.rmit.edu.au/dac/*
2 See *www.jesperjuul.dk/*, *http://ludology.org/*, *www.joystick101.org/*, *www.game-research. com/* and *www.digiplay.org.uk/*
3 See *www.gamestudies.org.*

THREE

DIGITAL GAMES AS CULTURAL INDUSTRY

OVERVIEW

Many books have been written on the digital games industry. Some focus on one company (e.g. Sheff 1993; Asakura 2000; Takahashi 2002), while, as we saw in the last chapter, others provide a very broad historical account (Herz 1997; Poole 2000; Wolf 2001; Kent 2002). Although useful, these texts do not provide us with an understanding of the structure of the industry, the relationships between the main players, and the relationship between the games industry and other industries. In addition, very little attention is paid to games for emergent platforms like mobile phones, the internet and digital television.

This chapter begins by situating digital games both conceptually and statistically within the wider economic and media environment. It considers how digital games might fit into what is commonly known within media studies as the cultural industries and it analyses the growing economic significance of the global games industry as compared with other cultural industries in major markets. It then moves on to examine the structure of the digital games industry and its key sub-sectors. Finally, the chapter examines two important trends in the industry, namely vertical integration and licensing.

This chapter adopts a theoretical perspective known as *political economy*, which was mentioned in the Introduction. Political economy differs quite fundamentally from orthodox economic theory. While there are different theoretical traditions within political economy, in general it is characterised by its holistic approach (which sees the economy not as separate from, but fundamentally linked to political, social and cultural processes) and its historical perspective.

Mosco (1996: 25) notes that a political economy of the media examines the structure and social relations which constitute the production, distribution and consumption of symbolic goods and is particularly concerned with the extent to which these social relationships may be unequal. Garnham (2000: 39) argues that political economy focuses on how power operates in the capitalist system and its 'effect on the structure and performance of the media system and on the relation between the producers and consumers of culture'. In this chapter a political economic perspective is applied to examine the contested relationship between development companies, independent publishers and hardware manufacturers/publishers. This perspective also serves to highlight the impact that increasing vertical integration and licensing are having on the ability of new entrants to enter the industry and on the diversity of games produced.

THE DIGITAL GAMES INDUSTRY AS CULTURAL INDUSTRY

'Cultural industry' originated as a critical and political term to describe the industrialisation of culture in the USA in the 1940s (Adorno and Gurevitch 1977; Adorno and Horkheimer 1979). For these writers the industrialisation of culture was the opposite of what culture was meant to do. They believed that culture was meant to offer a critique of everyday life and the prevailing political and economic system, not be a fundamental part of it. Over time the concept of the 'cultural industry' has become pluralised and shifted away from the view that industrialisation and commodification are in themselves a bad thing. The current focus is instead on how the capitalist system structures and influences the commodities that get produced. Within the political economy of the media, 'cultural industries' as a term signifies those institutions that are directly involved in the production, distribution and circulation of meanings via symbolic forms. With the increasing diversity of information industries, even this definition may now be too imprecise. However, in media studies, and in this book, the 'cultural industries' refers to the traditional media industries of television, radio, books, newspapers, magazines, film and music as well as the newer media industries of the internet and, I would argue, digital games. Advertising, marketing and education are also usually included (Garnham 2000; Hesmondhalgh 2002).

Can the digital games industry be conceptualised as a cultural industry? Any attempt to so define it must attend to the key features which have traditionally been seen to characterise the cultural industries and describe how these features operate in the digital games industry. From a political economy perspective, three features are especially pertinent in this context: (i) the high risk involved in cultural production, (ii) the high production costs but low reproduction costs of cultural products and (iii) the semi-public good nature of cultural products and services (Preston 2001: 231; Hesmondhalgh 2002: 17). Broadly speaking, the cultural industries have developed a number of strategies to respond to these features. Indeed, when one analyses these strategies, one begins to find a number of similarities between the traditional cultural industries and the digital games industry.

Only a small number of cultural products make a profit. These small numbers of 'hits' must cover the production costs of a large number of products which fail to make a profit. The primary reason for this level of risk is that consumer tastes in cultural commodities are driven by irrational factors like fashion and style more than need, and are thus highly unpredictable. A related reason stems from the status of cultural products as information and the fact that audiences need to sample an information good before deciding if they want to buy it or not. In order to cope with these consumption uncertainties, major cultural corporations produce a large repertoire or portfolio of products using a number of formulae that communicate clearly to the audience what they can expect from a product.

For example, in the film industry the production of films in easily identifiable genres serves as one formula to signal to the audience what type of pleasure they can expect from a particular film. The use of 'stars', 'serials' and 'trailers' are other strategies that attempt to reduce risk and thus overcome the high rate of failure. Similar strategies are evident in the digital games industries. It is estimated that only 3 percent of digital games make a profit and in an effort to introduce some similarity and predictability to the production process, publishers tend to commission games that fall into particular generic categories, as in the film industry. Another response has been to attach a licence to a game, that means that 'intellectual properties' from other media, or the real world, are used to create or 'pre-figure' certain expectations in the market. We shall explore this strategy in more detail later in this chapter. In addition, successful games increasingly spawn sequels, tie-ins and merchandise. Finally, as in the film and television industries, the digital games industry circulates playable demos and screenshots, especially through game magazines and websites, in advance of a game's release in order to communicate to their consumers the key features of a new product.

Within the cultural industries, the relative costs of production are very high when compared to the relative reproduction costs. For example, to produce a film master and to market that film is very expensive when compared to the relatively cheap costs of reproducing multiple copies of that film. In order to recoup these production costs, cultural industries have a strong incentive to maximise their audience. This translates today into a search for global markets, a desire to distribute the product across as many media as possible, and an attempt to control distribution channels. Analysis of the Hollywood film industry highlights the importance, for example, of overseas markets to that industry and the extent to which the film industry depends on broadcast television, DVD and video rental and retail for revenue (Wasko 1994; Hesmondhalgh 2002: 187–89). Similarly, within digital games a PC or console gold master can cost $3–10 million to produce and the same again to market. However, the reproduction costs of a game on CD are minimal and thus digital game publishers work to maximise global sales and to 'port' their games from one platform to another. Interestingly, this feature does not hold true for the entire field of digital games, as a subscription-based online game incurs ongoing production costs. Nevertheless it applies to the vast majority of games that are sold on CD or cartridge through standard retail outlets.

Throughout the cultural industries there is a strong tendency to integrate vertically and horizontally in order to control costs and ensure access to as wide a set of distribution channels as possible. Doyle (2002: 22) defines horizontal integration as 'when two firms at the same stage in the supply chain or who are engaged in the same activity combine forces'. She defines vertical integration as expansion 'either forward into succeeding stages or backward into preceding stages in the supply chain.' A third form of expansion is diagonal integration whereby 'firms diversify into new business areas'. In the film and broadcast industries in many countries, regulators have stepped in to control the extent to which companies may vertically integrate. The trend towards vertical, horizontal and diagonal integration is also evident in the digital games industry where publishers, in particular, are vertically integrating both upstream with developers and downstream with distribution companies as well as buying other publishers.

In addition, publishers are increasingly operating across gaming platforms and sectors, from PC to console and mobile. Companies like Vivendi also operate across a range of other media and non-media sectors. Vertical integration in particular will be examined in more detail towards the end of this chapter.

Finally, to define a cultural product as a public good is to point to the fact that it is not destroyed during use and can be reused by others who may not have to pay for it. This is a feature of many knowledge products, as Machlup (1984) noted. However, it does cause problems for producers in terms of how they are to recoup their investment in terms of creating the original, and costly, product. While the dissemination and copying of a cultural product may be almost costless, its original production certainly is not. This characteristic gave rise to the development of 'intellectual property rights' and 'copyright', which are monopoly rights afforded to a producer in return for their investment, and which effectively turn public goods into private goods (Garnham 2000: 58). The traditional cultural industries developed complicated ticketing, payment and collection systems and began to rely on advertising revenues to ensure production costs were covered. While there are marginal costs involved in increased sales in the digital games industry, as in the print industry, the industry has also developed both technological and institutional solutions which attempt to ensure that the publisher and the developer receive payment for their investment. There is a constant battle against piracy and hackers in the digital games industry, although recent examples whereby the source code for *Half-Life 2* (2004) was stolen and the Xbox and the N-Gage encryption systems were hacked, illustrate that these solutions are not entirely secure.

ESTIMATING THE ECONOMIC VALUE OF THE DIGITAL GAMES INDUSTRY

While clearly the digital games industry displays many of the characteristics of other cultural industries, how does it compare economically? Constructing an accurate picture of the size of the global games industry in terms of software and hardware sales is a difficult task, as estimates vary widely and do not remain accurate for long. Government, consultancy and press reports usually fail to give a global perspective on the industry and sometimes offer contradictory information, depending on their particular agenda. This section explores data commissioned by the following publishing associations: the Entertainment Software Association (ESA)[1] in the USA: the Entertainment and Leisure Software Publishers Association (ELSPA) in the UK; as well as government reports from the UK, Japan and South Korea.

While there have been dramatic collapses in the digital games industry over the past 30 years, particularly the 1983 crash in the USA, statistics over the past 10 years point to a steady growth in digital game sales, both in monetary and unitary terms, across all platforms. The rate of overall growth across all sectors of the industry is crucially tied into the console life cycle. Thus, just before the launch of a new generation of platforms (roughly every five years), the rate of overall growth in the industry slows as consumers wait in anxious anticipation of the new platforms and games. Indeed, in 2000 the overall value of retail sales shrank slightly and in 2001 remained weak with a growth of only 7 percent (Deutsche Bank 2002: 10). By 2002 the launch of the PlayStation 2 (PS2), the GameCube and the Xbox was having an impact on overall sales and this continued until the end of 2004, when the market slowed in anticipation of the next generation of consoles (DataMonitor 2002; DFC Intelligence 2004). In the first quarter of 2005 console game sales in the USA remained around 7 percent but overall sales in the American games market grew by 23 percent, driven by handheld hardware sales following the launch of Nintendo's DS and Sony's PSP (NPD Group 2005).

While hardware and software are intimately tied in this industry, it is useful to focus on software sales. A UK government report published in 2002 suggested that the global 'leisure software' industry in 2000 was worth approximately £13 billion, of which almost £10 billion was accounted for by games software (Spectrum Strategy Consultants 2002: 10). Within this total, the USA was the largest market with 35 percent of total sales, followed by Europe with 31.5 percent and then Japan with 18.5 percent. These figures are largely corroborated by figures published by Deutsche Bank in 2001 but this report estimated that the USA accounted for 40 percent of total sales followed by Japan at 33 percent and Europe at 26 percent. A third source estimated that total games software sales in 2001 were worth $17.7 billion and indicated that the largest market was the Asia Pacific market with sales of $7.6 billion in 2001 (DataMonitor 2002).

A more recent report estimates that the global games industry was worth $27 billion in 2002, of which two-thirds was accounted for by software. It expected the industry to decline somewhat in 2005 and

TABLE 3.1   Value of global software and hardware sales ($bn)

	Software sales	Hardware, software and peripherals	Sources
2002	18 billion	27 billion	Forfás 2004 report which draws on data from a variety of consultancy reports.
2003	21 billion		OECD 2004 report which draws upon a variety of sources.
2003	18.2 billion		Screen Digest report. Introduction available on the web. Figure refers to interactive leisure software which is broader than games.

then to accelerate to reach $30 billion by 2010 (Forfás 2004: 2). Another report estimated the industry to be worth $21 billion in 2003, although it is not clear if this figure includes hardware (OECD 2004b). A third source estimated that the global interactive software market was worth $18.2 billion in 2003 (Screen Digest 2004). The last three references draw upon consultancy reports to which this author did not have full access and so they are used with caution. It is not clear, for example, to what extent wireless/mobile games are included or the revenues for Asian markets. For industrial strategists, policy makers and academics the lack of independent and affordable data on the digital games industry makes strategic planning and rigorous comparison with other industrial sectors difficult.

So how big is an industry, which generates around $18 billion annually in software sales? These figures become more meaningful when we compare them to sales figures for other cultural industries. Unfortunately, there is no source which collates this data on a global scale but figures for the USA from a variety of trade associations provide an interesting basis for comparison. The Entertainment Software Association in the USA and the National Purchase Diary (NPD) Group, a consultancy based in New York, estimate that total sales of video and computer game software in 2004 generated $7.3 billion and when hardware and accessories are added, the total comes to just under $10 billion. By comparison, domestic box office in 2004 in the USA generated $9.5 billion (MPAA 2004). Interestingly, while growth in the

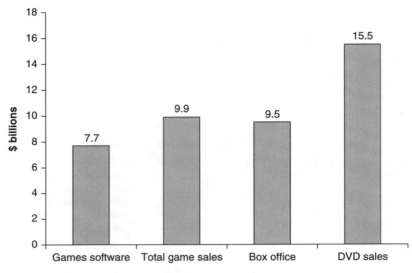

FIGURE 3.1   Sales of US entertainment media, 2004 ($bn)

Sources: Entertainment Software Association, National Purchase Diary, Motion Picture Association of America, Digital Entertainment Group. Accessed May 2005

digital games industry has been fairly steady over the past five years, growth in American box office and in domestic recorded music sales has been almost nil and declining respectively since 2001 as new formats emerge (ESA 2004; OECD 2004a). Meanwhile, growth in DVD sales has been accelerating and one source estimated that Americans spent $15.5 billion on DVDs and a further $5.7 billion on renting DVDs (DEG 2005). This figure does not include sales of DVD players.

The figure for 'total game sales' is often used to suggest that the digital games industry earns more revenue than the film industry. Indeed the claim is made so often in the popular press and game magazines that it demands closer investigation. What these comparisons usually fail to point out is that 'total game sales' includes sales of game hardware, accessories and leisure software, which is a very broad category of products. When we compare game software sales only to content only sales in other sectors, we get a more accurate picture. In addition, these comparisons often fail to explain that cinema receipts or box office form only a small percentage of the total revenues made by a film. Indeed, box office receipts account for just 25 percent of the total revenue of a film and typically video and DVD sales/rentals, network and cable TV and pay-per-view are all important additional sources of revenue (Deutsche Bank 2002: 29).

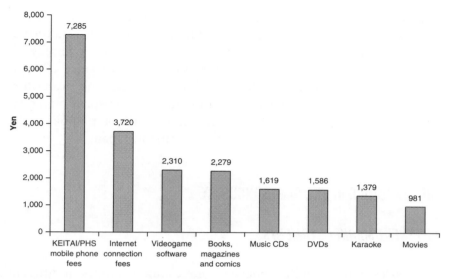

FIGURE 3.2 Average monthly expenditure on leisure activities in Japan, 2002
Source: CESA (2002: 90)

While these sales figures provide one means of comparing the economic value of digital games to other cultural industries, another way is to consider how digital games compare to other media in terms of monthly consumer expenditure. The Motion Picture Association of America (MPAA) found that in 2001 consumers spent most on television, with home video and books coming in second and third. Games were included in a category with interactive television and cinema box office and came fourth.[2] By comparison a survey of monthly expenditure by 1,000 people in Japan in 2002 on leisure activities found that people spent most on mobile phone fees, followed by internet connection fees and then videogame software. Fees for mobile phone and the internet of course could include payment for accessing online games. Books, magazines and comics came a close fourth (CESA 2002; see Figure 3.2).[3] Interestingly, spend per capita was greatest for DVDs, followed by mobile phone connection fees and videogame software. This reflects the slightly higher prices spent by lower numbers of people on these media.

The various figures and tables in this section have provided us with a lot of data. To summarise briefly, it would appear that while the digital games industry is growing in economic terms, it is still not as large in total value terms as some other cultural industries. Furthermore, total sales are vulnerable to changes in hardware, particularly in the console and handheld sub-sectors. Growth in the industry is nevertheless steady (at 4–8 percent per annum) and while this is impressive compared with cinema box office receipts in the USA since 2001, it should be measured against the growth of new emerging media formats to give perspective. Finally, the monthly amount spent on digital games is dwarfed by spend on television, home video and books in the USA and by the mobile phone and the internet in Japan.

THE STRUCTURE OF THE GAMES INDUSTRY

DIFFERENT MARKET SEGMENTS

Total sales figures tend to hide very interesting dynamics in different subsectors of the digital games industry. Dmitri Williams (2002) divides the games industry into three market segments according to the main hardware platforms: consoles, handhelds and personal computer (PC) and argues that each has its own underlying dynamics. Such a segmentation is applied widely in industry reports and in terms of sales, console games currently dwarf games sold for other platforms and constitute from 57 to 78 percent of total global software sales (DataMonitor 2002; Deutsche Bank 2002; Spectrum Strategy Consultants 2002). At present the main consoles are Sony's PlayStation 2 (PS2), Microsoft's Xbox 360 and Nintendo's GameCube (GC). Some reports group games for handhelds such as the Game Boy Advance (GBA) with the other console platforms.

Interestingly, not all markets demonstrate the same affinity with console games. While console games dominate in Japan, with almost 94 percent of total sales, this falls to 80 percent in the USA and 55 percent in Europe (Spectrum Strategy Consultants 2002: 10; ESA 2003). Europe is by far the largest market for sales of PC games, at 47 percent, followed by the USA at 35 percent (Spectrum 2002: 11). Sales of games on other platforms form only a small proportion of total revenues currently. However, the Spectrum report estimates that the mobile games market in Europe, the USA and Japan was worth £73 million in 2001, with Japan constituting over 50 percent of this total (2002: 15). They predicted that the mobile games market would double in value to 2005 and that the online games market would grow

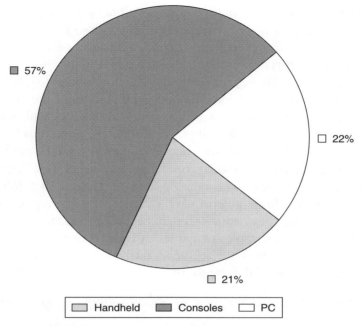

57%

22%

21%

Handheld   Consoles   PC

FIGURE 3.3   Global software sales by platform, 2001

Source: Deutsche Bank (2002: 5)

from £0.5 billion in 2001 to £0.89 billion in 2005. Other sources claim that online gaming will increase dramatically as broadband becomes more widely available, and point to the growth of online games in South Korea where broadband penetration is very high and online games constitute over 60 percent of the total domestic game market (KGDI 2004). It is anticipated that the next generation of consoles from late 2005 will all incorporate online capabilities.

In what remains of this section we will develop a slightly different market segmentation of the digital games industry. This segmentation takes games themselves, or what we might call the software aspect of the industry, rather than hardware as its starting point. Table 3.2 differentiates between four game segments: console games, standard PC games, massively multiplayer online games (MMOGs) and mini games.[4] There are two reasons why this segmentation makes sense. First, while sales of console, handheld and PC games are the most significant in terms of sales at the moment (see Figure 3.3), it is clear that other segments are emerging which offer alternative business models, new types of games and are attracting new types of gamers. Many industry reports pay only scant attention to these segments. Second, a hardware-based segmentation is unsatisfactory, given the tendency for hybrid and new platforms to emerge at relatively regular intervals. The development of MMOGs, for example, currently exploits the online capabilities of the PC to produce a new market segment with unique characteristics which are different from other types of multiplayer online PC and console games. Mini games like PC web downloadable games and puzzle/card games are currently played on personal computers, mobile phones, digital televisions and handhelds.[5] The development of systems like Infinium's Phantom, which will be able to play a variety of game types, suggests that platform-based segmentations may become redundant.

Table 3.2 gives examples of games in these four market segments and further outlines how the segments differ along the following four economic and industrial dimensions:

1 Market concentration – monopoly, oligopoly or numerous companies.
2 The revenue model – shop sales, online sales, subscription, pay per play, free, advertising.
3 Degree of openness in hardware system – open, mixed, closed.
4 Characteristics of the software production process – cost, length, team size.

Segment 1 includes games developed for both handheld and console platforms and is clearly the most significant in terms of market share at the moment (see Figure 3.3). These two platforms are combined into one segment because of their similarities across the different criteria in all but their storage device. This segment is often described as an oligopoly, with three platform developers involved in both hardware and software production: Nintendo, Sony and Microsoft, alongside a relatively small number of independent publishers.[6] While Nintendo have enjoyed a dominant position in the handheld market for a number of years, there have been a number of new entrants recently and Sony launched a competing platform, the PSP, in 2005. While one might describe the segment as an oligopoly, there is strong competition between the major players in this segment and previously dominant market players like Atari and Sega have found that having a dominant market share is no guarantee that one can keep it (Gallagher and Park 2002; Williams 2002).

TABLE 3.2 Key segments of the digital games industry

Segment 1 Console Games	Examples of Platforms and games	Market Concentration	Revenue Model	Openness of Hardware System	Software Production Process
1A	**Console/Video** *Final Fantasy* on PS2, *Halo* on the Xbox, *Donkey Kong* on the GameCube.	Hardware oligopoly Sony, Microsoft, Nintendo	Hardware developed as a loss leader and money made on sales of software. Games sold on CD through shops. Premium retail price. Many games now adding online and multiplayer functionality.	Closed. Proprietary and non-interoperable hardware systems.	Games expensive to develop, little follow-up service costs. Average length of dev. 18 months. Average team size 12–40.
1B	**Handheld** *Pokemon* on GBC, GBA, GBASP. Also *Gamepark, N-Gage* and *Zodiac*. Sony's PSP Nintendo's DS.	Until recently a Nintendo Hardware Monopoly. New entrants Nokia, Tapwave and Sony.	Hardware developed as a loss leader and money made on sales of software. Games sold on cartridges through shops. Premium retail price. Newer handhelds include multiplayer functionality.	Closed. Proprietary and non-interoperable hardware systems.	Games expensive to develop, little follow-up service costs. Average length of dev. 9 months. Average team size 12–20.
Segment 2 Stnd PC Games	**Examples of Platforms and Games**	**Market Concentration**	**Revenue Model**	**Openness of Hardware System**	**Software Production Process**
2A	*Harry Potter and the Philosopher's Stone, Quake, Black and White, Diablo II &* *battle.net*	Numerous.	Games sold on CD through shops. Many games now adding online functionality and downloadable elements. Cheaper retail price than segment 1.	Common standards, non-proprietary technology.	Games less expensive to develop than console & handheld. Average length of dev. 15 months. Average team size 12–15.

(Continued)

TABLE 3.2 (Continued)

	Examples of Platforms and games	Market Concentration	Revenue Model	Openness of Hardware System	Software Production Process
Segment 3 Massively Multiplayer Online Games	*World of Warcraft Blizzard/Vivendi Lineage II/NCSoft.*	Oligopoly EA, Sony, Microsoft, NCSoft, Vivendi.	Games sold on CD through shops but played online. Consumers pay monthly subscription fee and online service charges to a telecoms operator.	Common standards, non-proprietary technology. Developed mainly for PC.	Very expensive to develop and significant ongoing costs.[7]

	Examples of Platforms and games	Market Concentration	Revenue Model	Openness of Hardware System	Software Production Process
Segment 4 Mini/ Games					
4A	Internet Microsoft's The Zone, Sony's The Station.	Numerous players including the major players in other segments.	Advertising used to support free games distributed via portals on the internet. Also pay per play and monthly subscriptions.	Common standards, non-proprietary technology.	Inexpensive to develop and small teams.
4B	Mobile *Snake, Frogger.*	Numerous players. DoCoMo in Japan, Sprint in the US, also Sega and Sony.	Games sold online and pay per download model. Revenue divided between developer and operator.	A number of competing proprietary technologies.	Inexpensive to develop and small teams. Average length of production 6 weeks–3 months.
4C	Digital Television PlayJam in the UK and CableVision in the USA.	Numerous players.	Games channels offered as part of a digital subscription package. Advertising an important revenue source as is SMS and telephone calls.	A number of competing platforms and input devices.	Inexpensive to develop and small teams.

Segment 1 is marked by the fact that console games are played on a small number of proprietary, closed and non-compatible technological systems which are upgraded every four to five years. Hardware life-cycles are a unique characteristic of this segment, whereby every four to five years the major platforms are upgraded and often changed so fundamentally that they impose not only an extra cost on the consumer but also a steep learning curve on developers, who must strive to produce games which harness the particular technological strengths offered. Gallagher and Park (2002) identified six distinct generations of console platforms between 1976 and 2002. In each generation hardware systems usually offered little backward compatibility. In this regard Sony's PlayStation 2 broke with tradition.

The oligopolistic nature of this segment, combined with the closed technological systems has a strong structuring effect on the software production process and means that the major platform developers erect a number of barriers in order to protect their market share and prevent the entry of competitors. Thus while games can be 'ported' from one platform to another, the main platform developers go to great lengths to control the flow and quality of content onto their system and to ensure that non-licensed software from non-accredited developers will not work on their platforms.

Nintendo, for example, is well known for introducing both a hardware solution (the 'lock-out' chip), and an economic/management solution, namely high and strictly controlled licensing fees, to control the production of console games for its platforms. Indeed, across all the platforms in this segment publishers/developers must pay a licence fee on every game sold to the platform developer, which is estimated to add $7 to $10 to the total cost of a console and handheld game. In some cases they must also pay the platform developer to manufacture the software. In addition, all the platform developers impose stringent quality control, known as Technical Certification Requirements (TCRs), on publishers/developers before they will allow a title to be released on their platform. Furthermore sometimes they want exclusive rights to a title so that it will only be available on their platform. These extra fees and barriers help to offset the hardware production and marketing costs incurred by the platform producers and help to keep the price per unit of each game high.

The core business strategy adopted by the platform manufacturers in the console segment is to sell their hardware as a 'loss leader' in order to build market share and to rely on the sales of software to make their profits (Alvisi et al. 2003). This pricing strategy is similar to that adopted by manufacturers of razors, who sell their razors at a loss but make their money back on the sale of razor blades. If the platform developer succeeds in building a large installed base, then they can make generous profits on their software and in turn reduce the cost to the consumer of their hardware, which should in turn spur sales of software. The relationship between hardware and software in all segments of the digital games industry can be defined as 'complementary'. However, in Segment 1 of the industry, the development of competing proprietary technology systems means that in order to build market share, each system must exploit these complementarities and create 'switching costs' to stop people buying alternative systems and products. Thus while market share is dependent upon the sale of consoles, console sales are directly related to the number of high-quality titles available for the console.

Console games are sold at a premium price through specialist and non-specialist shops and are generally distributed as CDs, DVDs or cartridges and packaged in boxes or jewel cases. While retailers currently constitute an important stage in the value chain (see Chapter 4), an interesting development is the growth of console games with online functionality, which may over time reduce the role of the retailer in the value chain. To date both Sony and Microsoft have launched networks to support online multiplayer play – PS2 Network Gaming and Xbox Live – allowing users to play against other players online and to download additional game content. The continued development of online functionality may ultimately lead to more downloads and less high street retail, although a key barrier to this in many markets is the lack of broadband availability.

Segment 2 includes most PC games but not MMOGs. In contrast to Segment 1 this segment has a much smaller market share, particularly in Japan and the USA. While this might prove a disincentive for some developers, for others, the smaller market share is outweighed by the cheaper development costs, given that PCs/Macs are based on common standards and open architectures. In addition, developers do not have to pay a licence fee or royalties to the platform manufacturer. These facts are reflected in a cheaper retail price than for a console game. The downside of this openness is that there is greater competition. Williams (2002) notes that there were 4,704 PC titles available in 1998 compared to 44 for the Nintendo 64 and 399 for the PlayStation. PC games are generally sold as boxed CDs through specialist and non-specialist retail outlets, although many companies release upgrades and patches, i.e. software that fixes bugs, online.

Despite the fact that console and PC games have both been developing online elements, MMOGs are marked by specificities which require classification as a separate segment; not least the fact that they are persistent games with ongoing production and customer service costs. It is difficult to estimate market share as general industry reports do not separate out MMOGs from standard PC games; but many reports would recognise the potential of this segment, particularly when one examines how things have developed in the Korean market, which has one of the most highly developed broadband networks in the world. At the same time it is important to remember that console gaming was banned in Korea until relatively recently and, as such, online PC gaming developed in a rather protected market. Other countries are unlikely to follow the same pattern.

Segment 3 can also be described as an oligopoly, as a small number of large companies like NCSoft, Vivendi Universal and Sony are involved in the development, publishing and distribution of the most successful (in subscription terms) MMOGs including *Lineage II* (2004), *World of Warcraft* (2004) and *Final Fantasy XI Online* (2002) (Woodcock 2005). However, the main platforms are currently open platform, as in Segment 2, and mainly based on PC and internet common standards. Developing a persistent world requires significant investment not only in initial development but also in ongoing costs including maintenance, expansions and community support.[8] Kline et al. (2003: 161) note that *Ultima Online* (1997) took two years to develop, was beta-tested with 25,000 players, and that support staff cost one million dollars annually. Industry interviews have suggested initial development costs of approximately €15million. Despite a number of high-profile game cancellations last year, the sector is still growing and attracting significant venture capital investment (Shamoon 2005). This may have something to do with the fact that while most MMOGs are sold on CDs through shops, the consumer must also pay a monthly subscription fee of up to $15 and ongoing telecommunications charges to play in the world.

The final Segment, Segment 4, covers the development of mini games for platforms such as digital television, mobile phones, PDAs and the Internet. Again overall market share and value are difficult to determine, but a recent ESA report estimated that while less than 10 percent of games played online were MMOGs, just over 13 percent

IMAGE 4 *World of Warcraft* ® (2004) image provided courtesy of Blizzard Entertainment, Inc.

were browser-based mini games and almost 55 percent were puzzle/ card based games (ESA 2004). This segment is embryonic but in general is characterised by shorter development cycles and lower production costs than the other segments. There are numerous players in this segment and a mixture of open and proprietary technologies. Competition is fierce, margins are low, and technical interoperability problems abound.

In Segment 4 there are a number of revenue models including: pay per download, pay-per-play and advertising. For example, most telecom operators offer users access to mobile games on a pay-per-play or pay-per-download basis. In most cases developers are not paid a cash advance and rely on a share of the revenues generated by the game – a share which varies from operator to operator and territory to territory. In Japan the i-Mode model adopted by NTT's DoCoMo is generous and content developers may receive up to 90 percent of revenues. In Europe the revenue share obtained by developers varies widely from a low of 20 percent to 50 percent. In the USA the rate is closer to 80 percent (TerKeurst 2003). Interestingly, some mobile developers have indicated in interviews that as mobile handsets improve, mobile games may start to be sold through specialist and non-specialist shops.

Mini games are also available via the internet and digital television. Often these games are provided free on game portals and the service is supported by advertising; or people are charged not to play but actually to upload their score onto a leader board. Another development is 'advergaming', which is the development of free games which are paid for in advance by a client in order to advertise a particular brand, for example, *The Nokia Game* (1999). Advergaming as a concept is sometimes used to describe the development of product placement in games, as the use of Red Bull power-ups in *Worms 3D* (2003) and *Judge Dredd: Dredd vs Death* (2003) demonstrates (Edge 2004a).

It is clear from this analysis that the console and the PC segment operate according to what Bernard Miège (1989) called the 'editorial model' of production, whereby the publisher finances creative development largely through direct sale to the consumer and the main problems are managing creative personnel and the uncertainty of demand. Interestingly, Segment 3 appears to be developing a mixed editorial and flow model, whereby initially there is a need to sell product direct to the consumer but in addition there is a need to supply an ongoing support and content service to consumers, and quality and speed of distribution is key.

CASE STUDY: MICROSOFT

While the four game segments identified above operate according to quite different dynamics, some companies operate in more than one segment of the market. Microsoft, for example, currently has a presence in all four of the segments.

When Microsoft entered the games industry, it developed and published standard PC games (Segment 2) and one of its biggest hits in this market was *Flight Simulator,* launched in 1983. With the launch of the Xbox in 2001, Microsoft moved into both hardware manufacturing and into the console segment of the market (Segment 1). The company moved to exploit online play in 2002 with the launch of Xbox Live, which allows players of console games to access a closed subscription-based service which enables multiplay over broadband networks.

Microsoft also publishes the MMOG *Asheron's Call,* developed by Turbine Entertainment Software Corporation from Boston. In addition, the company has ongoing interests in interactive television/ WebTV and distributes free web games on *The Zone* on their online service, MSN.

Microsoft's move into different market segments can be seen as an attempt to broaden the company's portfolio of software products in order to offset market risk and overcome uncertainty over future business models and delivery platforms. The company's move upstream into hardware and downstream into online distribution signals the company's desire to control distribution direct to the home and to challenge the market share of Sony and Nintendo.

Further sources of information: (Takahashi 2002), www.xbox.com, www.xboxlive community.com/www.microsoft.com/games/ac/, zone.msn. com/en/root/default.htm)

THE PRODUCTION CYCLE

One can also analyse the digital games industry in terms of the actors and their role at different stages of the production cycle. The core stages in the production of games software are design, pre-production, production, publishing, distribution and retail. Although these stages vary in duration and type from market segment to market segment, the procedure is largely similar. Variation does occur in the MMOG segment, where there is a requirement for ongoing community support and content development following retail.

IMAGE 5 *Flight Simulator (2004): A Century of Flight (2003)* image provided courtesy of Microsoft.

The Spectrum report (2002: 9) likens the production cycle in the games industry to the film, music and book industries. In all these industries, a publisher provides an advance to a creative artist and on completion of the work, takes on the role of marketing and distributing it. Once costs have been recouped, the artist receives a percentage of royalties. A similar process takes place in the console and PC segments of the digital games industry, although 'the artist' who develops the game is usually a team of people. Further, 'the artistic' or production stage is increasingly integrated into the publishing stage in the games industry and game ideas today are just as likely to originate from the publisher as elsewhere, reflecting what Williams (1981: 52) has called the 'corporate professional' structure of cultural production. Thus, while in the book and music industries the creative stage remains largely independent from the publishing and distribution stages, increasingly in the digital games industry design and production are conducted by salaried staff within publishing companies. Furthermore, as we shall see, in the major global companies the first three functions of the production cycle are increasingly vertically integrated and controlled by one company.

There are three types of development company:

1 *first-party developers* or internal teams which are fully integrated into a publishing company;
2 *second-party developers* who are contracted to create games from concepts developed by a publisher;
3 *third-party developers*, or independent development houses, who develop their own projects and try to sell them to a publisher.

The extent of first, second or third party development varies from country to country but one source suggests that today close to two-thirds of game production is done by first-party developers (Williams 2002: 47). In other words, a majority of games are developed by teams working within, or owned by, a publisher.

Publishers regularly get a bad press in the industry trade magazines and websites. Horror stories of projects being canned for no particular reason and royalties being withheld do nothing to dispel such beliefs.[9] However, interviews with people in the industry provide an equal number of stories of development companies who lack adequate management structures and cannot complete a game on time or within budget. Certainly publishers are the bankers of the games industry and since they incur all the risk and uncertainties involved in such an investment, they adopt an aggressive and tough approach to negotiations with, and management of, developers, particularly start-up third-party developers. At the same time it is often rarely understood by start-up developers that publishers fund portfolios of projects across the different genre categories and if their portfolio of games in production has enough FPS games then no new project in this genre will get funded, no matter how good the idea. Further, once a project is funded, most publishers play a role in the overall management of the production process because they must be able to schedule the game into their localisation, testing, manufacturing and marketing pipeline.

During the 1990s, Cornford et al. (2000) found that the global publishing industry consolidated around 'a core of between 10 and 20 major publishers', including well-known companies like Electronic Arts, Nintendo, UbiSoft, Infogrames/Atari and Take2. At the same time, fears that the industry would consolidate even more have not been realised and the new trend is towards vertical integration with developers rather than merging and acquiring other publishers (DFC Intelligence 2004). TerKeurst notes that the top publishers now run 'round-the clock, round-the-globe production' with development teams recruited or established in different locations based on labour costs, specialist skills (for example, racing and FPS), and localisation/marketing needs. Many publishers also own their own distribution channels, almost 80 percent according to one estimate (Deutsche Bank 2002: 26), and so this stage in the cycle is often fully controlled by the publisher.

The retail stage of the production cycle is more and more the preserve of large supermarkets and specialist chains, particularly in the USA where Wal-Mart and Best Buy dominate. In Europe independent retailers still constitute a significant part of the retail sector. As the main access point to consumers, retailers can significantly influence the success of a game through their allocation of shelf space and in-store marketing. As supermarkets and specialist chains grow in size, they acquire more power to negotiate discounts on wholesale products and returns to publishers. Retailers often charge publishers market development funds (MDF) to cover the cost of posters, end-of-aisle space and other services. They may also force the publisher to bear some of the discounting costs associated with games that do not sell well (Williams 2002). One source estimates that retailers earn a gross margin of 35–40 percent on a full price

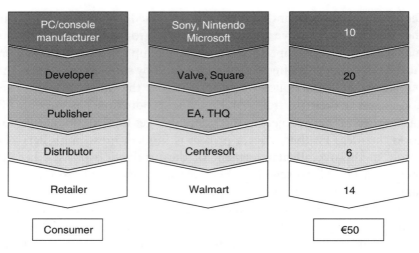

FIGURE 3.4   The digital game value chain
Source: Deutsche Bank (2002: 18)

product (Deutsche Bank 2002). While variations on this production cycle exist, the majority of games follow these production stages.

The production cycle can also be conceptualised as a value chain, whereby at each stage of the production cycle companies add value to the core product and contribute to the final price paid by the consumer. Figure 3.4 outlines the different players in the production cycle and estimates, in the column on the right, how much each player in the console value chain adds to the total cost paid by a consumer for a game.

KEY TRENDS IN THE DIGITAL GAMES INDUSTRY

Different industry reports tend to highlight different trends in the digital games industry. The Spectrum report (2002) notes that production costs are rapidly increasing and that there are an increasing number of platforms. The Deutsche Bank report (2002) also singles out the rising production and marketing costs as a significant trend, but highlights the fact that publishers are consolidating and that digital games are increasingly being sold by non-specialist retailers. They foresee that next generation 'convergence' consoles will provide multiple entertainment options. More recent reports again point to increasing consolidation in the industry but also the growth of middleware and the increasing number of licensed games and sequels in the top ten best-selling games (Forfás 2004). In the space that remains, this chapter will briefly analyse the trend towards consolidation and licensing in the games industry and trace these trends back to a key feature of the cultural industries, the high risk of failure involved in the production of a cultural product whose success depends on highly volatile factors like fashion and individual taste.

CONSOLIDATION: VERTICAL, HORIZONTAL AND DIAGONAL INTEGRATION

While early histories describe the games industry as a cottage industry with individuals able to program a game in a matter of weeks, the reality of the industry today is far from this. In the console and MMOG segments, we noted that oligopolies have emerged whereby a small number of very large companies dominate the market. While it is true to say that there is fierce competition between the main players (Gallagher and Park 2002; Williams 2002), in the current console lifecycle Sony's installed base of PS2s at over 100 million, dwarfs Nintendo's 8 million and Microsoft's 6 million. This generation of consoles might be called the 'Age of Sony' were it not for Nintendo's success in the handheld subsegment with the Game Boy Advance (GBA) and no-one's willingness to underestimate Microsoft. History has shown us that the market leaders in one generation will not automatically become the leaders of the next.

An analysis of trends in the digital games industry across all the market segments finds that the dominant business strategy is vertical integration up and down the production cycle alongside a degree of horizontal and diagonal integration, as companies attempt to expand into different market segments. The imperative behind these forms of integration is the need to exploit 'economies of scale' and 'scope', to maximise global sales and to control distribution. These trends are not unique to the digital games industry, as Hesmondhalgh (2002) points out in relation to other cultural industries in general, and the experience of Disney in particular. What is of interest from a political economy perspective is the impact that these business strategies are having on (i) the ability of new players to enter the market, (ii) the diversity of products produced, and (iii) the costs of products to the consumer.

We have already seen that the main platform developers, like Microsoft, operate across all stages of the production cycle and are investigating moves into retail through subscription services, pay-per-play and downloads. We have also seen how the current organisation of production means that the supply of console games is strictly controlled by the platform manufacturer and the procedures they have put in place means that console games are sold at a premium price through specialist shops. These business strategies have already come under scrutiny by national and supranational organisations for their anti-competitive tendencies. Sheff (1993) details a number of instances when Nintendo was taken to court in the USA for anti-competitive practices and currently the European Commission, under pressure from the International Software Federation (ISFE), is investigating whether or not Sony has placed a limit on the numbers of games it will publish on its platforms and if this contravenes competition law.

The dominance of the platform developers/publishers in the console segment and the fact that reproduction costs of games are relatively low have encouraged other companies to adopt business strategies aimed at maximising economies of scale. The past decade has seen many third-party developers go out of business and those who remain have attempted to increase the scale of their operations and/or integrate both upstream and downstream (Cornford et al. 2000; Pham 2001; Kerr and Flynn 2003). Publishers, in particular, have been forced to increase in scale in order to maintain some control in the production cycle vis-à-vis the platform manufacturers and increasingly large retailers. They have done so by buying each other, acquiring distribution channels, and buying into (or taking over) development studios. Ownership of development brings two benefits: a means of maintaining control over production and deadlines (Cornford et al. 2000) and a means of retaining more of the revenue from game sales. Publishers may also acquire development studios in order to gain access to intellectual property, for example, the purchase by Infogrames of Shiny Entertainment for $47 million in 2002 to obtain exclusive publishing rights to *The Matrix* film licence.

Interestingly, and despite the dominant trend towards consolidation, there is some evidence to suggest a countervailing tendency, at least with regard to development studios. A number of cases have arisen where publishers or platform developers have bought development companies only for the core of that development team to leave to start a new company, because they felt that their creativity was being compromised in the larger corporate structure (Cornford et al.

2000; CESA 2002; Edge 2003a, 2003b). A well-known example of this occurred when *Black and White* designer Peter Molyneux famously left his company Bullfrog when it was bought by EA and founded a new company called Lionhead Studios.

Scale alone is often insufficient to offset the risk and costs involved in developing a cultural product, and analysis of the games industry also finds that many companies are exploiting what is known as 'economies of scope'. Doyle (2002: 14) defines economies of scope as 'economies achieved through multi-product production' or variations on existing products. Economies of scope are a fundamental means by which the media industries more generally, and publishers in particular, reduce uncertainty of demand. We have noted that production costs have been steadily rising in the digital games industry across all the segments while at the same time only a small number of games make a profit. As a result publishers tend to develop a broad catalogue or portfolio of titles across genres and platforms in order to ensure they have at least one successful title. They also tend to develop sequels to games and where possible to reuse core technologies. This strategy is found less in development studios, which tend to specialise in the production of particular genres of games, but even here we find the evolution of 'super-developers' in the USA and the UK, which comprise four or five different teams working simultaneously on different projects. Economies of scope are thus fundamentally linked to economies of scale, given that one needs scale in order to distribute a wide range of products to the largest market possible.

LICENSING

A further trend which seems to be accelerating in the digital games industry and is certainly exercising many speakers at international games conferences is the increasing use of licences. A licence gives the owner the right to use a certain intellectual property (IP) in certain ways in their game. While initially licences were very limited and games might only use the licenced IP in the packaging and marketing of a game, increasingly licenses include the rights to use the voice and likeness of the main characters in a game, and in some cases the production of a game may proceed alongside the production of, for example, the film, whose licence it will use. This occurred in the case of the *Enter the Matrix* (2003) game.

TABLE 3.3 Top 10 selling console games in the USA, Jan–June 2003

Title	Publisher	Developer	Developer Type	Licensed IP	Sequel
Zelda: Wind Maker	Nintendo	Nintendo	In-house	No	Sequel
Enter the Matrix	Atari	Shiny	In-house	Yes	New
The Getaway	Sony	SoHo	In-house	No	New
GTA: Vice City	Take 2	Rockstar North	In-house	No	Sequel
The Sims	EA	Maxis	In-house	No	Sequel
NBA Street Vol. 2	EA	EA	In-house	Yes	Sequel
Def Jam Vendetta	EA	AKI Corp	Independent/ third party	Yes	New
Tom Clancy: Splinter Cell	Ubi Soft	Ubi Soft	In-house	Yes	New
SOCOM	Sony	Zipper	Independent/ third party	No	New
Dragon Ball Z	Bandai	Bandai	In-house	Yes	Sequel

Source: Forfás (2004)

Licensing is a strategy which publishers and developers use to overcome the uncertainty of demand for games because of, what film historian Thomas Schatz has called, their 'pre-sold' properties (Schatz 1993). Kline et al. (2003) note that drawing on pre-existing IP reduces marketing costs because the most expensive element, that of building awareness, has already been done. From real world properties like David Beckham or Tony Hawk, to television properties, like Starsky and Hutch, to film properties like *The Matrix* it would appear that licencing is becoming more ubiquitous. Sports licences are also an important feature of sports games, adding considerably to their perceived realism and sales. Screen Digest found that in 2000 'licence-based titles accounted for 45 percent of allformats in the UK top 100, up from 28 percent in 1997 and 42.5 percent in 1999 (Screen Digest 2001)'. Table 3.3 would suggest that the trend is continuing, particularly in the console segment.

Four things stand out in Table 3.3. First, half the games are based on licences and only two of the new titles are non-licensed IP. Second, only two of the developers are third-party developers. Third, half of the titles are sequels. Finally, of the top ten selling console games in the USA in the first six months of 2003 only one, *SOCOM*, was based on original IP and developed by a third-party developer.

One argument that could be made here is that increased cross-media licencing helps to increase sales and broaden the market by providing themes, narratives and characters that non gamers are already aware

IMAGE 6 *SOCOM: US Navy SEALs* (2002), image provided courtesy of Sony Computer Entertainment Europe.

of. Certainly, both developers and publishers currently feel that the addition of a licence increases their chances of, first, getting a publishing deal and, second, reaching a large enough market to make a profit. A political economy perspective however suggests that the increasing interdependence between media products in different media industries may lead to a reduction in the overall diversity of texts and the scope for radical innovation to emerge (Wasko 1994). It would also suggest that the growth of licences, combined with consolidation in the digital games industry, is making it increasingly difficult for new entrants and independent developers to operate (Kerr 2003a, 2003d; Kerr and Flynn 2003). Given that only one of the top ten selling games in the console segment of the market in the USA in 2003 was developed by a third-party developer, and this was based on licensed IP (*Kingdom Hearts* (2002) developed by SquareSoft), the signs are not good.

It is clear that the digital games industry is now an important part of the wider cultural industries. Looking beyond the data, we can see that the industry is far from uniform. Indeed, we find a number of competing technologies and business models, and while the console segment currently dominates in terms of sales, MMOG and mini games provide interesting alternative business opportunities. In addition, markets are far from uniform with, for example, sales of console games dominant in Japan and the USA while online PC games and MMOGs dominate in Korea.

As the industry matures, companies in the digital games industry are adopting a range of business strategies to reduce their investment risk and increase their returns. These strategies have much in common with the strategies adopted in more traditional cultural industries. In this chapter we have focused on just two: increasing consolidation and the increasing use of licences. Both these trends suggest that there is decreasing space for small and/or independent publishers and developers, and consequently, fewer opportunities for original game ideas to make it to the marketplace, especially in the console segment of the market. Political economic analyses of older media industries suggest that these two trends are linked, and that increasing concentration will over time lead to less diversity in terms of the range of content available. Notwithstanding the appearance of some original titles, if we examine the top selling games across all platforms this suggestion appears to have some resonance.

Finally, it is worth noting that while the digital games industry has professionalised and many of the companies have grown into global companies, there is a constant need for innovation, creativity and new games. Even after an intense period of vertical integration and large-scale licencing, there is still recognition within the industry that third-party developers or small-scale independent operations could produce the next *Half-Life* or *GTA*. In this regard one cannot ignore the contribution of modding groups and fans and companies like Valve and Maxis have been keen to foster relationships with these groups (Postigo 2003). A weakness with much political economic work to date is that it focuses on the formal market while tending to ignore the work of academics, artists and user/fan groups which operate on the fringes of the market. While the goods that these groups produce may not be formally bought and sold, they may nevertheless contribute to overall innovation and diversity in the industry. This aspect of the games business will be examined in more detail in Chapter 5.

SUMMARY

This chapter has established that the digital games industry displays many of the characteristics of more established cultural industries. It has shown that while growing in economic terms, the digital games industry is still less significant than such industries as television, recorded music and DVD sales. The chapter noted that the industry is internally diverse with the console and PC segments operating somewhat like the book publishing industry and the MMOG segment operating more like the broadcasting industry. Finally, we found that increasing concentration in the console segment, coupled with the erection of high barriers to entry, was resulting in less original console games, more licensing and more sequels.

NOTES

1 The ESA was formerly known as the Interactive Digital Software Association (IDSA).
2 Total number surveyed = 1,013. Different numbers of people responded to each leisure activity.
3 Unfortunately, television and VHS were not included in the CESA survey.
4 This segmentation could be extended to include arcade games. While this has not been a core focus of my own work, and is almost totally ignored by most industry reports, it remains a significant revenue stream for companies like Sega, Capcom and Namco and an important source of IP for budget 'nostalgia' games and mini games.

5   Indeed, one possible implication of Microsoft's XNA development platform might be that players will be able to play some games across, console platforms.
6   An oligopoly occurs when a market is dominated by a few large suppliers.
7   One source estimates that EverQuest costs $10 million annually to run. See http://www.gamespy.com/amdmmog/week3/
8   Even if the gamer logs out the game continues, or persists.
9   One industry source told me that almost 70 percent of funded projects get canned at some stage during the production process.

FOUR

GLOBAL NETWORKS AND CULTURES OF PRODUCTION

OVERVIEW

While the last chapter examined the structure, dynamics and overall trends in the digital games industry, this chapter explores how a game gets made and the negotiations and crucial determinants influencing the production process. A key trend within the last ten years has been the increasingly global nature of the games industry. In this chapter we will examine how publishing companies headquartered in LA, London and Tokyo interact with globally dispersed hardware, development and supplier companies. The focus then shifts to the production cycle and production cultures in development companies. While one individual may create the vision for a game, the production of a game is a team-based process shaped by many individuals, the working culture and crucially the relationship with a publisher. Finally, we explore the role that the game player plays in the production process either explicitly, as designer or as tester, or implicitly, through market research and online communities; and we highlight the problems that these channels pose in terms of reaching non-hardcore players and more global markets.

The focus in this chapter is on Anglo-American production cultures although where possible we refer to Asian production cultures. For reasons of space, this chapter will focus on the console and PC segments of the industry primarily. The data presented was gathered in face-to-face interviews with developers and publishers in the UK and the USA over a period of five years and analysis of industry magazines and websites.

GLOBAL NETWORKS OF PRODUCTION

The period since the 1970s has been characterised by immense social, economic and political change. In *The Rise of the Network Society* Manuel Castells (2000) argues that the new economy that emerged was based on information, globalisation and networking. He writes about the demise of mass manufacturing in the 1970s and the emergence of a new organisational logic which manifests itself in a range of flexible organisational forms in the 1980s (2000: 164). For Castells, the network is the fundamental organisational logic of contemporary economies and information technology enhances that logic. Even if one disputes the notion of a new economy, it is clear that corporate organisational forms have been shifting, multiplying and extending their reach globally even while corporate ownership has been consolidating.

Few academics have examined the global organisation of production in the games industry and what little research there is comes from very different perspectives (TerKeurst 2002; Kline et al. 2003; TerKeurst 2003; Tschang 2003). Kline et al. (2003) describe digital games as the ideal commodity of post-fordist, information and promotional capitalism (2003: 62). Post-fordism in their book refers to three shifts in society: from mass industrial production to small-scale flexible production structures; from mass consumption to more fragmented, niche markets; and from the welfare state to deregulation. 'Information capitalism' describes a shift from the production of material goods to the production of information goods and the increased emphasis placed on innovation (2003: 66). 'Promotional capitalism' describes the growing importance of promotion and marketing in contemporary societies (2003: 68–74). Certainly, the digital games industry is globally distributed, based on flexible production networks, targets niche markets and is largely unregulated. However, I would argue, it also demonstrates a complex complementary relationship between material and information goods which is often ignored in contemporary accounts of information capitalism and, while there are increasing levels of promotion, marketing and publicity, publishers seem to lack the tools and information to enable them to understand non-traditional (i.e. non-hardcore) consumers both in established and in newly emerging markets globally.

For decades now, the digital games industry has operated internationally and major companies have established subsidiaries outside their home markets. This trend was driven by Japanese companies like Sega and Nintendo who sold their products into the American market in the 1980s. However, with the entry of major global conglomerates like Sony and Microsoft into the industry in the 1990s we see increasing pressure on independent publishers to consolidate and organise their production and distribution networks on a global scale. If we analyse the digital games industry today we find a clear correspondence between the location of the main markets in the USA, Japan and Europe and the location of the headquarters of the main publishing companies in LA, New York, London and Toyko. Both publisher-owned and independent development companies are much more dispersed around the world in developed economies in the USA, Europe, Asia and Australia/New Zealand and increasingly in countries in Eastern Europe and in Canada. Moreover, the firms that manufacture game hardware and accessories are located in developing economies and free trade zones in Mexico and China.

Thus, while the digital games industry has experienced conglomeration, consolidation and vertical integration in the past decade it has also built a complex range of global networks of production. In the console subsector, the major players have outsourced the reproduction of CDs and console production from places like Silicon Valley to Mexico in an attempt to exploit cheaper labour, shorter distances to major markets, and just-in-time inventory management structures (Herz 1997: 113–117; Kline et al. 2003: 205–9). Microsoft's Xbox is manufactured, under licence, by Flextronics in Guadalajara in Mexico and in Hungary, while Nintendo has extensive manufacturing operations in Brazil (Takahashi 2002: 197). While these reproduction structures are driven in part by the desire to take advantage of more flexible specialisation in production, it is clear that deregulation and the transnational free-trade agreements, including the North American Free Trade Agreement (NAFTA), and lower levels of legal and labour control also play a role.

The organisational trends are somewhat more complicated in the development and publishing sectors of the industry and across the different segments in different countries. Chapter 3 argued that a key trend in the publishing sector of the console, PC and MMOG segments of the digital games industry were increasing scale and both vertical and horizontal integration (Cornford et al. 2000; Deutsche Bank 2002; Spectrum 2002; Williams 2002; Kerr and Flynn 2003). While many large publishers outsource, there is a countervailing tendency to bring key aspects of the creative process in-house. Indeed, the primary motives behind acquiring a development studio are access to key intellectual properties and/or to obtain greater control over the creative process. Publishers sometimes leave development teams to act relatively autonomously once they buy them (for example, when Microsoft bought Ensemble studios). However, in many cases publishers increase their levels of involvement in an acquired development company over time, as happened when Liverpool's Psygnosis was bought by Sony. The end result is greater control over the creative process, deadlines, deliverables and revenues.

In addition to purchasing development studios around the world, publishing companies are increasingly establishing local offices in their major markets. While the headquarters of each corporation is still located in the company's home country these subsidiaries deal with consumer-orientated functions like marketing and localisation and usually employ a small number of local staff who manage a larger number of contract staff. Thus, Electronic Arts (EA), which is an American company and is headquartered in California, has international development and marketing subsidiaries in Australia, Austria, Brazil, Canada, France, Germany, Hong Kong, Switzerland, Taiwan, Thailand and the UK. Atari, which is now a French company with its headquarters in Lyon, has subsidiaries in North America, Europe and Asia Pacific. Konami, a Japanese company, is headquartered in Tokyo and has subsidiaries in the USA, the UK and Hong Kong (DataMonitor 2002).

Given the increased concentration, scale and global reach of the publishing sector, independent development companies have had to increase in scale, professionalise and specialise in order to survive. Increasingly employees have had to specialise in particular roles and development teams have begun to specialise in particular game genres. We have seen the emergence of super-developers in the USA and the UK with five or more teams working on different games simultaneously. Interestingly, while many development studios are located in remote locations, in order to take advantage of lower labour costs, they are not moving to the same low-cost, low-tax locations as manufacturing elements of the industry. Clearly the need for skilled labour is an issue here. Research in the UK has found that most of the core development functions are still done in-house with only 'non-core' functions like localisation, porting games from one platform to another, adding music and voice-overs and the production of full motion videos (FMV) being outsourced (Cornford et al. 2000: 92). This may change with the next generation of technology when the anticipated rise in production costs may encourage more outsourcing and indeed off-shoring, but it does not appear to be the norm in the current generation.

Much more empirical work needs to be done before we can make definitive statements about the organisation of the games industry at a global level. What we can say, based on the available evidence, is that game production, particularly in the PC and console subsectors, is increasingly concentrated and controlled by a small number of large companies who through acquisitions, subsidiaries and outsourcing overcome very real geographic, technological, cost and cultural barriers to production, distribution and retail. This industry also provides an interesting example of the persistent and intricate relationship between information goods and services and material goods. In the next section we will explore the production process in more detail by examining the various stages in the process and the complex linkages and balance of power between development companies, hardware manufacturers, publishers, retailers and the players of digital games; all players in the global digital games production network.

THE PRODUCTION PROCESS

The USA, Japan and the UK are the main centres of digital game software production and all have substantial numbers of people employed both directly and indirectly in the digital games industry. In the USA the ESA estimates that almost 30,000 people are employed in digital game development and publishing with a further 195,000 indirect jobs in the information, trade and transportation sectors (IDSA 2001). In Japan game hardware and software employs an estimated 30,000 people (Aoyama and Izushi 2003). In the UK the digital games industry employs more than 20,000 across all sectors, with 6,000 employed directly in game development (Spectrum 2002: 20). A more recent survey estimated that 9,400 worked in game development (Skillset 2004). Other growing centres of game development include South Korea, Australia and some countries in Eastern Europe.

The stages of the production life-cycle were mentioned in the last chapter and include design, prototype, pre-production, production

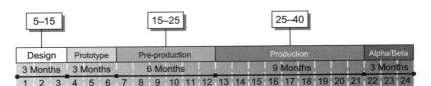

FIGURE 4.1 Production stages and increases in staff on an average 24-month project

Source: Torc Interactive

and testing. Figure 4.1 outlines the increasing numbers of staff required to move from pre-production into production on a console or PC title. Production begins with design and prototyping work, which is done by a small core team, and this is then used to obtain finance or approval for the project. Pre-production involves more advanced production and design work, and production is when the team expands to its largest staff numbers and includes both alpha and beta testing. In what follows we will examine these stages in more detail from the developer's perspective in order to better understand the factors that shape the production process and how the end user becomes involved.

DESIGN AND PROTOTYPE STAGES – THE SEARCH FOR FINANCE

The design and prototype stage of the lifecycle is dominated by negotiations between the development company and its financiers. While certainly part of this stage involves generating an innovative game concept, it would be foolhardy not to realise that the primary goal is to sell the game concept to a publisher, secure a financial advance, and negotiate hard to retain a good percentage of the intellectual property rights and the royalties. The pre-development stage of the production cycle can, for many companies, take many months.

All games begin as a concept or proposal briefly described on a few pages of paper. A game proposal usually includes information on the core idea – including the genre, environment, artwork and music/sound – and also the target platform, market and budget. Ten years ago a game proposal might have been sufficient to persuade a publisher to fund a project, but today an advanced technical prototype must also be produced. This can mean significant investment by the development company in advance of securing money from the publisher. This demo is crucial to the negotiation of a publishing/distribution deal, particularly for start-up third-party companies who must demonstrate not only the core idea but also their capability to deliver. While demonstrating the core strengths of the game idea is what the developer is mainly concerned with in pre-production, the publisher is also concerned with market competition in that genre, fitting a new game idea into the schedule of games they currently have in the production pipeline, and the developer's track record. Indeed, the publisher may request that certain aspects of the core idea be changed before they agree on a design document and a financial deal.

As in the traditional media industries, a developer with an established reputation is perceived as less of a risk and they can negotiate a larger advance and a higher percentage of royalties. For start-up third-party developers, publishers will agree to advance $1–3 million for a good idea but often include a 'claw-back' clause whereby if the project is canned for any reason, the publisher can demand their money back, which may effectively wind up the development company. Start-ups usually receive either a lower royalty rate than established developers or a variable royalty rate, whereby once a minimum number of sales have been reached then the royalty rate goes up.

> [It may] look like you got an incredibly good deal [but] the agent or publisher owns everything, owns the technology, owns the IP, even though you have designed it yourself ... effectively you have got nothing, no assets in the organisation ... you have just got the ability of the staff in your organisation. So if you are a newbie and you are just glad to get a deal you tend to be asked to sign away your life and if ... no-one else is competing for you then what are you going to do? (Interview 1, Former employee of a publisher)

Obtaining the funding to develop an advanced demo is a significant hurdle for small third-party developers. Many third-party developers pursue venture capital funding and exploit private sources. Some third party developers are developing alternative funding sources. For the sequel to *State of Emergency* (2002), Vis Entertainment Plc in Scotland created a special function company funded by shareholders. In some countries game-specific venture capital funds – for example, the Fund4Games in the UK – have been established. In France, the government has extended the brief of the existing film funds to enable game companies to apply for funding to develop game prototypes

(Kerr 2004). The aim is still to get a publishing deal but, particularly for start-ups, finding a way to reduce the 'perceived risk' associated with investing in their project is crucial. The more developed one's game is, the lower the risk from the publisher's perspective.

> We've found getting to the publishers relatively easy. What we have done, which is of big benefit, is to completely take them out of the circle of game development, so that has made it a lot easier for the publishers to approach because we are taking the risk out of it. We are not looking for them to give us development money. (Interview 14, third-party start-up)

What the developer is trying to do at this stage is to secure sufficient funding to cover the actual costs of development and have something over to cover the costs involved in developing a demo of their next project. The average development cost of a console game is approximately €5 million but some games cost considerably more – MMOGs cost at least double this – and the addition of a film, book or sports licence will also increase the costs. Sometimes developers will pre-pay for the rights to a licence and use this as leverage in their negotiation with publishers. Sometimes the publisher will already own a number of licences and require the developer to alter their design document to facilitate it. Regardless of who owns the licence, intellectual property rights are becoming an increasingly important part of developer–publisher negotiations (Kerr and Flynn 2003). Figure 4.2 outlines some of the costs involved and the potential range of companies involved in the production life-cycle of a console/PC game.

Choosing the target platform(s) for one's game is a crucial decision as it affects the design and technologies used to develop the game, as well as the partners and channels one must negotiate with. It will also influence the total number of sales needed to break even. A PC game is cheaper to develop and because one does not have to pay a royalty on each game to the console manufacturer, PC games have a lower break-even point. The Spectrum report (2002) estimated that in 2002 a PC game which had received a £1 million advance would have to sell almost 230,000 units to repay the advance before it could make a profit. This is a significant rate of sales to achieve. The PC market is relatively small and the lower barriers to entry mean that there is intense competition for shelf space, with more than twice as many PC titles released annually compared to console titles. In 2001 in the USA almost 2,500 PC titles were released and of these only 68 sold over

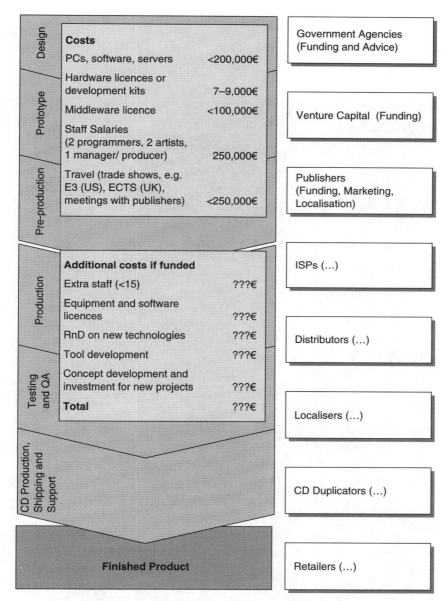

FIGURE 4.2 Costs and companies potentially involved in the production of a PC or console game.

100,000 units, only 10 sold over 300,000 and only 5 sold over 500,000 units (Deutsche Bank 2002: 41). These figures would suggest that very few made a profit.

IMAGE 7 *NBA: Inside Drive* (2004), image provided courtesy of Microsoft.

TABLE 4.1 Publisher-funded and self-funded business models on a PC title

Game Funding	Publisher advances £2.5m	Self-funded
Ave. wholesale price	£14	£14
Royalty %	25%	40%
Royalty £	£3.50/unit	£5.60/unit
Unit sales	**Receipts to developer**	**Receipts to developer**
150,000 (low)	nil	£840,000
300,000 (medium)	nil	£1,680,000
600,000 (high)	nil	£3,360,000
1,200,000 (super high)	1,700,000	£6,720,000

Source: www.gamesinvestor.com. Accessed 8 June 2005

Choosing to develop for one of the major console platforms means that the developer must pay the hardware manufacturer a licence fee and acquire a specific development kit. Even after the game is completed, they must still submit the game to the console manufacturer for final quality approval before it can be released. While the console market is the largest market segment, a console title costing $2.4 million to develop and with a cash advance of $1.6 million from a publisher would have to sell 250,000 units to recoup the advance and return a profit to the developer (Deutsche Bank 2002: 19). Clearly if one has the capital, then self-publishing is the ideal because one obtains a higher percentage of royalties, one recoups more of the costs earlier, and the break-even point is lower. Table 4.1 illustrates this point. If a developer receives an advance of £2.5 million and the game costs that much to develop, they will not see any profit until they sell 715,000 units at £3.50 a unit. If the game is self-funded, the developer starts to makes money on all sales.

The design and prototype stage of the production cycle is quite different for first party/internal development teams as compared with third-party companies. Internal teams are informed in advance that there is a slot available in a publishing schedule for a particular genre of game aimed at a particular market segment. This means that they do not need to make a business case for a game and do not have to guess what type of game the publisher might want – two important challenges faced by third-party developers when they pitch a game idea to a publisher.

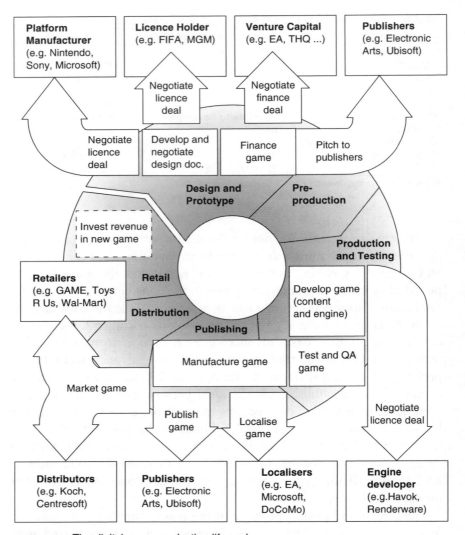

FIGURE 4.3   The digital game production life-cycle

PRE-PRODUCTION, PRODUCTION AND TESTING

The pre-production and production stages of the life-cycle take 15 months for a console game on average, while PC games are somewhat shorter and mini games can take less than a month to complete. The development of a digital game is a complex process and involves the timely and well-managed flow of work between artists, designers and programmers. If a company spends too long on the game engine, for example, then the art and gameplay may be underdeveloped and vice-versa, if too long is spent on the art, then the underlying technology will contain 'bugs' and not be well integrated. Much of the trend towards vertical integration in the digital games industry has been driven by the perceived need for more project management, more 'personality' management and more time for testing products.

Having secured a finance package, a number of key challenges must still be faced by a game development team/company, some of which will be internal to the company, and some external. The first is to make sure they have the skills and resources in place to ensure timely delivery of their product within budget. The second is to make sure they are informed as to forthcoming technological changes but also that they monitor any potential changes in the publishing sector and in the market.

Once a publishing deal or sufficient other forms of finance have been secured, and there is an agreed design document with the pub-lisher, the development team will expand either by redeploying staff from within the same company or by taking on extra staff on contract. The size of development teams can vary widely, depending on the type of company. However, a team of 12–25 people is average for a con-sole game with at least half of these engaged in content development and design and the remainder in programming and management (Tschang 2003). Again there are variations from country to country. In game development companies in Japan, where there are sufficient resources to justify a separate research and development team, the content and design complement of development teams is higher (70–80 percent). Also in Japan only a small number of people are ded-icated to each project, which then draws upon the skills of in-house specialist teams as required, for example, full motion video (FMV) producers (TerKeurst 2002). These specialist teams move from project to project and their time is managed so that they are rarely without work. In game development companies in the UK, where the average company size is 22 employees, project teams are self-contained and each team has all the skills needed to complete a project. While addi-tional skills are hired or subcontracted out, it is quite common for staff in UK companies to experience periods when their services are not required.

Figure 4.4 illustrates the core roles involved in a production team, including producers, designers, artists and audio specialists. The core

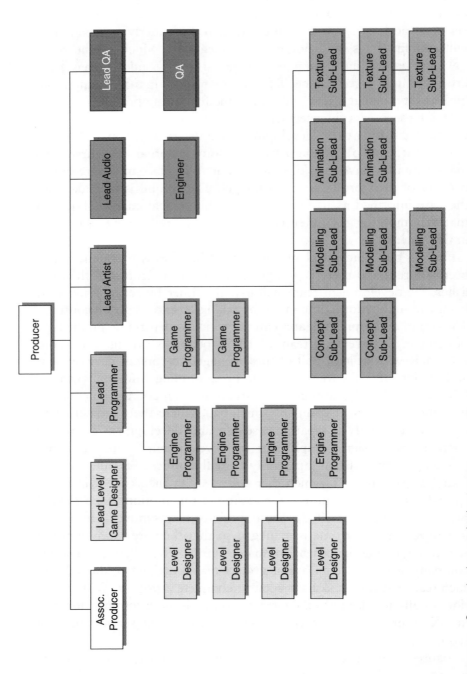

FIGURE 4.4 Core roles in a production team

Source: Torc Interactive, Personal Communication, 2004

function of the designers is to establish the look and feel of the game, which involves designing the core gameplay mechanics – including multiplay – the levels, the characters, the environment and lastly the story. The artists are involved in 3D design (modelling and animating characters and environments, and deciding on lighting and cameras), 2D design (the graphical user interface) and FMV for the cut scenes. The programmers are involved in animation, physics, artificial intelligence (AI), tool development, scripting and back-end programming. The producer role varies depending on the company but often this person has responsibility for managing the entire production pipeline (scheduling, budgeting, hiring of resources) and carefully monitoring slippage in any of the different elements of the technology/engine, design or content development. If one element of this process takes too long, this will have severe knock-on effects on the other elements, which cannot be implemented or tested until the underlying technology is in place. The producer/associate producer is usually involved in monitoring progress, developing contingency plans and communicating with their publisher.

Where once people in the digital games industry were largely self-taught, more and more people enter the industry with general degrees in computer science, animation and art or more specific qualifications in game design and technology. 'Hard skills' in programming (C++, physics, maths, AI, Direct X) and art and design (3D Studio Max, Maya, Photoshop) must usually be supplemented by 'soft skills' in teamworking, communication and problem solving (DTI 2001; Preston et al. 2003). Many of these skills are transferable from other industries although a few, such as game design and knowledge of particular development environments, are highly specific to the industry. Often companies will also look for a passion for games, talent and game industry experience, or a significant amateur game modification (modding) portfolio.

Experience is the 'holy grail' and experience gained while working on a commercial product, or a successful modding project, is how people get jobs and how development companies get publishing deals. Increasingly the names of top programmers and designers are becoming known to consumers as well: for example, Will Wright, designer of *The Sims* (2000), Hideo Kojima, designer of *Metal Gear Solid* (1998), Shigeru Miyamoto, designer of *Donkey Kong* (1983) and *Super Mario Bros* (1985), John Carmack, programmer on *Doom* (1993) and *Quake* (1996). Producers, by comparison, are relatively

TABLE 4.2 Hard and soft skills required for major roles in games development

Role	Programmer	Artists	Games Designer	Producer
Hard skills	1. Maths or physics Programming – C, C ++ 2. Software packages – assembler, direct 3D, TCP/IP, Windows, Win CE, DirectX, Java, J2ME, OpenGL 3. Specific platform experience – PS2, Xbox, GameCube, GBA	1. Art and design skills 2. 3D graphics package –3D Studio Max, Maya, Softimage 3. 2D packages – Photoshop, Paintshop Pro	1. Model and character building skills 2. Basic programming skills 3. Basic 3D design skills 4. Freehand drawing skills	1. Software project management
Soft skills	4. Teamwork 5. Time management 6. Problem solving 7. Game industry experience 8. Passion for games 9. Talent	4. Teamwork 5. Communication skills 6. Visualisation skills 7. Game industry experience 8. Passion for games 9. Talent	5. Extensive knowledge and passion for games 6. Game industry experience 7. Communication skills 8. Presentation skills 9. Talent	2. Game industry experience 3. Extensive knowledge and passion for games 4. Communication skills 5. Presentation skills 6. Team management skills
Typical qualifications	Degree in computer science or game technology.	Degree or Diploma in Animation or Art	No specific qualification but diploma in game design course helpful	No specific qualifications but some training in project management a benefit.

Sources: DTI (2001), Preston et al. (2003)

unknown and probably have the least defined and broadest skill set. Historically, many programmers and artists got promoted into producer and project management roles which they were ill-equipped to fulfil (TerKeurst 2003). Project management was defined by one interviewee as:

> the [ability] to set milestones and achieve them in a harmonious way which doesn't allow the programmers or artists the licence not to make them. Project management is a big issue, the need to balance creativity and deadlines. (Interview 17, Industry association representative)

Development companies are increasingly using a type of software called middleware to reduce the amount of time it takes to program a game and save on research and labour costs. One approach often used by larger studios is to reuse the engines of previous games developed by the studio. One problem with this approach is that most engines are optimised for particular genres of games and thus the engine from a racing game will not reduce the development time of a role-playing game significantly. Another approach is to license a commercial game engine, such as Criterion's Renderware, which provides a flexible suite of tools optimised for most genres of game and for cross-platform development. Criterion's Renderware includes tools for AI and physics programming and games like *Grand Theft Auto: Vice City* were built by RockStar North using this engine. The UnReal engine is a first person shooter engine, which has been used in *America's Army* and *Tom Clancy's Splinter Cell*, although intriguingly it was also used in *Harry Potter and the Philosopher's Stone*. Add-on middleware can provide additional real world physics capabilities, for example *Havok 2*. A licence for a commercial engine like UnReal costs $350,000 per game, 3 percent of royalties and a further $50,000 if the game is ported to other platforms. However, older engines and educational versions of engines can be downloaded free and are used by modding groups, students and start-up developers who want to learn the tools of the trade.

PRODUCTION CULTURES

Working on a digital game involves meeting milestones during the production period and the delivery of a gold master, on time, to the publisher. Poor project management and company management has led to many stories of poor working conditions in game companies. Kline et al. (2003) describe workers in this industry as 'net slaves' and note that 'management harnesses youthful technophilia to a compulsive-obsessive work ethic, one-dimensional character formation, and a high rate of burnout' (2003: 200). Another survey of the working conditions of 1,000 game developers in the industry noted the negative impact that long hours, extended 'crunches', 'forced workaholism' and job insta-bility had both on the industry and on family life (IGDA 2004). The answer they felt lay in better project management, better contracts, better human resource management and more family-friendly practices. Other research has pointed to the impact that such working conditions may have in terms of dissuading females from working in the industry (Kerr 2002; Ray 2004). By comparison, TerKeurst (2002) found excep-tional levels of project management and staff retention rates in Japanese game development companies.

Clearly there are interesting differences between the American/ British production cultures and their Japanese counterparts, at least in relation to project and people management. It is unclear to what extent these working conditions apply in Europe more generally, although one publisher noted that it was impossible to run development com-panies in some Western European countries because of their strong labour laws. It is an issue which the International Game Development Association (IGDA) and other industry bodies are keen to address.

Another aspect of the culture in development companies is the fact that it is male dominated, to an even greater extent than the wider ICT industry. A 2004 survey in the UK found that of 9,400 people work-ing in the games industry, only 8 percent were women (Skillset 2004: 14–15). This contrasts with 38 percent female participation in the media industry and 46 percent participation in the UK workforce as a whole. Anecdotal evidence suggests that many of these women are working in marketing, public relations and administration (Haines 2004). It would appear that this fact is not unique to the UK. Attempts by the IGDA to encourage more women into the industry and to set up a special interest group on 'Women in Game Development' have met with limited success. A press release issued by the IGDA in 2003 found that:

> The number of women employed in the game development industry is thought to be dramatically low, probably between 5 and 15 percent. …
> It appears that the percentage of women game developers has shown

very little growth over the past several years. Though programmers are only one of many game development roles women may fill, it is notable that, according to ACM, the percentage of women currently graduating with computer science degrees is going down. (www.igda. org/committees/women.php)

RELATIONSHIP WITH PUBLISHER

Another set of challenges faced by development companies relates to managing their relationship with the console manufacturer (where relevant) and their publisher. In the console segment of the games industry, the big three (Sony, Nintendo and Microsoft) compete against one another for market share. Each platform has a unique mix of technological characteristics and each platform transition sees the manufacturers carefully choosing which characteristics will win them competitive advantage. A key component of the mix is having sufficient games which demonstrate these unique characteristics. Console manufacturers work with first, second and third party development teams to ensure these characteristics are properly demonstrated but each new generation puts immense pressure on development companies to upskill.

The available evidence would suggest that while the platform manufacturers and publishers work hard to develop new technological innovations they are less willing to take a risk on a content innovation. In the last chapter we saw that, with a few notable exceptions, publishers are increasingly averse to any major reworking of genres and styles, preferring tried and tested formulas, licences and sequels. This viewpoint is supported by the proportion of licences and sequels in the top-selling all-format games. One report notes that internally EA tolerates 'not more than one high risk element per project' (TerKeurst 2003: 10). While Gallagher and Park (2002: 80) found that historically technological innovation was an important, but not sufficient, strategy for survival in this industry. Nevertheless, the console life cycle, and the technological innovations each new cycle introduces, has an important structuring influence on the design of games.

From a developer's perspective, each console generation requires considerable research and development to enable them to begin to harness the technology's potential and begin to think about how it might be used in future games. Developers must begin midway through the current cycle to research what new features might be included on the next generation of consoles (for example, online features, parallel processors) and to gain access to an early 'prototype'. The following quotation from a programmer in a medium-sized third party company illustrates the difficulties involved in shifting from the PlayStation to the PS2:

> We naturally assumed as we had made PlayStation One games that we would make PS2 games. So we got a development kit … and after a couple of months, a month or two of our lead programmer looking into it, he did a report … which said the PS2 is a very very difficult machine to program for and we were also hearing that from other developers anyway. What Sony did with the PS2 was they made a very powerful machine but they made a very low-level machine, so to get the most out of it you really have to get your hands extremely dirty and well really get down to the machine level, which is odd because most development is moving higher level, where you don't have to get down to the nitty-gritty machine code … we have all this PlayStation One experience but practically none of that hardware experience can be carried over to PS2. (Interview 2, programmer)

Technological change and the dangers of technological 'lock-in', in other words finding oneself with an out-of-date set of skills, are a very real challenge for game developers in terms of preparing for future projects, but may also influence projects already in development. If console games take 18–24 months on average to complete, then companies will only be able to make two games in each cycle. Further, if a game overruns, they may need to rethink some of its gameplay and core design elements in order to compete with next generation games. Confounding Factor's *Galleon* has been in development for seven years and this has meant redoing their graphics (because they started to look 'out of date') and rewriting their engine, because it was running too slow. While originally a PC only game, it was then mooted to be in development for the PS2 and Dreamcast and was finally released in 2004 as an Xbox game (Edge 2004d).

Another factor which development companies must take into account is the quality approval and testing procedure of the console manufacturer. While one aim of this procedure is to ensure that the game is bug-free, another is to ensure that the game meets certain technical and content standards and is compatible with the platform's marketing strategy. Both Nintendo and Microsoft have in-house

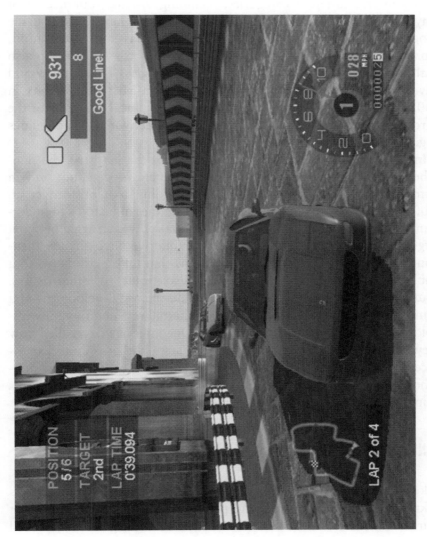

IMAGE 8   *Project Gotham Racing 2* (2003), image provided courtesy of Microsoft.

expert testing teams which provide developers with optional advice on their games prior to the final approval stage. Microsoft's in-house team in Redmond is called the Advanced Technology Group (ATG), while Nintendo's is called the Mario Club. The Mario Club scores games in five different categories, including visuals, sound, ease of play, game composition and overall satisfaction. They also rate game progression, accomplishment and reward, player customisation, replay value, originality and immersion. Microsoft's ATG group also evaluate play, art, audio and cross-regional issues. This team would have worked closely with the launch games on Microsoft's Xbox in 2001 to ensure they demonstrated the core graphical strengths of the hardware (e.g. *Halo* and *NFL Fever*) and its networking capabilities (e.g. *Project Gotham Racing*).

In both the console and the PC segment of the industry, the publisher plays a significant role in the development process, not only in terms of providing a cash advance. According to Cornford et al. (2000) the key to understanding the digital games industry is to understand the contested relationship and unequal power struggle between large publishers and small developers. While we have already mentioned the contested financial negotiations that take place between a publisher and developer, developers also point to other issues. Sometimes publishers go out of business during the development of a game, place projects on hold because of internal restructuring, or withhold payments for a variety of reasons. One interviewee recalled how they had released a game with a particular publisher only to experience direct competition in the same genre from another product published by the same publisher. Others had experienced their publishers going out of business mid-development.

CONFIGURING AND UNDERSTANDING GAME PLAYERS

A key issue for game developers, publishers and console manufacturers is knowing the varying tastes and patterns of demand across different markets. While we know that an American Football game will not sell in Europe and that Japanese dating games rarely make it to the West, certain titles like *Pokemon* sell globally. Indeed it appears that Japanese games sell better in the West than Western games sell in Japan. In 2003 only five of the top 100 selling Japanese games were developed in the West: *Ratchet and Clank, James Bond 007: Nightfire, The Lord of the*

Loan Receipt
Liverpool John Moores University
Library and Student Support

Borrower Name: Carter,Evie
Borrower ID: **********0116

The business and culture of digital games :

31111011565270
Due Date: 14/12/2012 23:59

Total Items: 1
11/12/2012 16:20

Please keep your receipt in case of
dispute.

Rings: The Two Towers, Metroid Prime and *Enter the Matrix* (Edge 2004b). A panel at the Korea Games Conference in 2004 noted that Koreans found the lighting in many Western games too dark and they considered the game characters to be ugly. In some cases Western games were too technically advanced to run on the PCs in the local internet cafes.

Few small to medium-sized game development companies conduct market research during the design, prototyping or development stages of game development, relying instead on feedback from testers, on sales information and on their publisher. Research conducted by Kerr (2002) found that small, third-party developers relied on an intuitive sense of market demand built upon a personal knowledge of competing products on the marketplace and personal preferences in the initial design and prototype stages. This would appear to correspond to Akrich's concept of the I-Methodology and it is a strategy that is increasingly being challenged by the requirement to move beyond hardcore gamers and exploit new market demographics, like women and older gamers, and to move beyond one's home market. Relying too much on intuitive design can result in games that only satisfy the hardcore gaming segment of the market and serve to exclude others.

This observation is supported by a recent study of game design in Norwegian development companies. Gansmo et al. (2003) interviewed a number of game development companies and found that masculine fantasies dominated design discussions. Furthermore when female players were discussed, a very traditional feminine 'stereotype' was evoked, which translated into game designs built around social relations, romance, emotions and role-playing. Gansmo et al. argued that there was very little understanding about how design might be linked to gender socialisation or of the variations between female game players. Indeed, they discovered a prevailing attitude that if females did not like to play existing games, then that was not the developer's problem. Academics would argue however that digital games are a 'prime example of the social construction of gender' and may significantly influence people's attitudes towards and use of computers in school or later career choices (Cassell and Jenkins 1998: 37).

It is worth noting that some companies have tried to reach beyond the hardcore male market, both by addressing the gender structure internally in their companies and by conducting extensive market research into female cultures, tastes and expectations. In the USA during the 1990s a number of female-owned and largely female-staffed companies like Purple Moon, HerInteractive, Girl Games and Girltech developed games for the female market (Cassell and Jenkins 1998). They also attempted to develop alternative market and retail channels for their products. Will Wright's Maxis has 40 percent female employees, a flexible and family friendly working environment, and produce games that are popular with females (Ray 2004: 161–2). While improved gender balance in a company will not automatically lead to games that prove successful with females, it is clear that women are under-represented in the industry at present.

Purple Moon closed after six and a half years and eight titles, including a soccer game for girls called *The StarFire Soccer Challenge*. Reflecting on her experience at Purple Moon, Brenda Laurel (2001: 4) noted that 'good research is never done' and that people are changing all the time. Driven by an agenda to understand teenage girl culture, Purple Moon employed both quantitative and qualitative research methods to inform their design principles and product development. This use of research is quite different from traditional market research used by most publishers and was an interesting attempt to explore potential rather than existing users.

Publishers today rely more and more on traditional market research, testing with 'expert users' and sales/registered user data to decide what works, what sells and to whom. Microsoft, for example, conducts multinational research on trends and game genres (TerKeurst 2003: 11). Most publishers meanwhile employ thousands of hardcore or expert testers to de-bug games prior to release (Takahashi 2002: 317; Kline et al. 2003: 203). What this research tells them is that their core market is male, ranging from 13 to 25 years of age. There is a clear tension between the publishers' desire to satisfy this articulate and accessible market and their desire to grow the market and invest in new markets, new genres, new design strategies, alternative marketing strategies and non-standard retail channels. This tension influences rates of innovation across all levels of the industry, from the decision about which games to fund, to the marketing of those games and the underlying platforms.

Market research surveys are relatively blunt instruments and tend to gloss over cultural differences and to reinforce gender stereotypes. An interesting example of such crudeness is provided by a study of the launch of the PS2 in 2000 and the redesign and launch of the PS One by Sony (Kerr 2003b). After two years on the market, 6.7 percent of PS2 registered users were female across the PAL territories[1] – a level

IMAGE 9 *Eye Toy: Play* (2003), image provided courtesy of Sony Computer Entertainment Europe.

which one Sony employee suggested was quite high. Interestingly, when the PlayStation was repackaged as the PSone, the percentage of female registered users for this platform rose from 10 to 20 percent, despite the fact that females were not specifically targeted in the marketing and advertising campaign. Sony felt that the new smaller design and the new price point were crucial to this change. What is noteworthy about this study in the current context is the fact that females are less inclined to buy games hardware than males, but little is known about the reasons for this. Second, market research is often carried out on the registered user base and since this is dominated by male console owners, little is found out about female game players, let alone female non-game players.

If one analyses the marketing and advertising campaigns of the console manufacturers and the publishers, it is clear that the target market is largely male. Acclaim's *BMX XXX* (2002) is just one example of blatant game content and marketing which targets a male, 18–34 market, but its poor sales should signal the dangers involved in such an approach. Nintendo's marketing campaigns for their Game Boy Advance SP initially used the tagline 'for men only'. Sega admits its marketing is all about 'testosterone' (Kline et al. 2003: 257). When a new console is launched, the high price and limited range of games mean that the main marketing message is clearly aimed at male hardcore gamers. Over time, as the installed base grows, the message is widened to a broader market, as evidenced in Sony's 2003/04 media campaign launched halfway through the console cycle, entitled 'Fun anyone?' Coinciding with the launch of the EyeToy it is a clear move away from the PS2 launch campaign built around the concept of the 'Third Place' and gritty black-and-white, David Lynch-directed ads.

Marketing to hardcore male gamers is what the digital games industry knows best. While mainstream marketing of games is arguably trying to maintain a gender-neutral approach, one only needs to attend any industry event or flick through an industry magazine to be confronted by a stream of images of women, cars and guns and an adolescent male discourse about them. This form of 'hegemonic heterosexual masculinity' can be traced back to the origin of games in male-dominated laboratories. Indeed, despite the feminist entrepreneurs of the late 1990s, and the efforts of the IGDA, what Kline et al. (2003) call 'militarised masculinity' pervades right throughout the production cycle. This is not to ignore developments like Sony's *EyeToy: Play* (2002), which are clearly aimed at non-hardcore gamers. However, the industry production culture is still dominated by males and heterosexual masculine fantasies, and the industry itself is at best ambivalent about the fact. In the next chapter we will see how these production cultures influence game cultures.

SUMMARY

This chapter examined how the digital games industry extended its production networks on a global scale in the late 1990s and the early part of this decade. We examined the production process and explored the contested relationship between third party independent developers and publishers. Finally, we examined a raft of challenges faced by developers, ranging from management issues and the lack of women working in the industry to dealing with constant technological change and struggling to broaden and understand different markets.

NOTE

1   PAL stands for 'phase-alternating line' and is a colour encoding system used in broadcast television systems in many countries in the world except the Americas, some East Asian countries, parts of the Middle East, Eastern Europe and France.

FIVE

DIGITAL GAME PLAYERS, GAME PLEASURES AND PLAY CONTEXTS

OVERVIEW

The last two chapters examined the structure and industrial organisation of the digital games industry and the process by which games get made. We noted the implicit and explicit roles that game players fulfil in the production process: from the designers themselves being game players, to user testing and market surveys. In the production and marketing process the primary market is clearly the 'hardcore' player, although increasing attention is also paid to the 'mass market'. In this chapter the focus is firmly on trying to go beyond the market data and implicit assumptions to explore who actually plays digital games, where they play, and the varying pleasures of digital game play.

In many business models and value chains retail is represented as the final stage in a linear process. However, Du Gay et al. (1997) argue that production and consumption should be thought of as a circular process of interconnected stages and not as discrete stages in a linear process. In the last chapter a diagram of the production lifecycle of a game (see Figure 4.3) delineated the relationship between producers and consumers. This signalled that the production process does not end with the retail of the game, but rather that retail feeds back into the development of new projects and is another source of innovation and knowledge for producers (Coombs et al. 2001; Haddon and Paul 2001). Retail can also be conceptualised as the beginning of the consumption process.

Consumption studies more generally and audience studies more specifically have opened up the 'black box' of the home and contributed to a greater understanding of the process by which consumers understand advertising and appropriate goods into their everyday lives (Mackay 1997). This process is variously referred to as 'consuming', 'shaping', 'appropriating' or 'decoding' in the literature. Political economy, social and cultural theory all agree on the fact that despite the best efforts of producers, designers and marketing companies, users or consumers are far from uniform or predictable. While producers may develop preferred functions, roles and meanings for users, or attempt to 'configure' them (Woolgar 1991), both theory and research suggest that the user, in different contexts, may interpret and use goods in diverse ways.

Where the literature diverges is in the degree of freedom, or agency, that they ascribe to users. While some work celebrates the autonomy of the user and sees consumption as a productive process (Fiske and Watts 1985; Fiske 1992), other work highlights the role that the producers, social structures and context play in constraining user agency (Bourdieu 1994; Garnham 2000; Hesmondhalgh 2002). For example, political economy argues that production puts 'important determining constraints on what is consumed, by whom, under what circumstances' and that media use is primarily determined by income (Garnham 2000: 115). Audience studies of how the media are used in the home point to the mediating role of relationships and the domestic economy (Silverstone and Hirsch 1992; Ang 1996; Silverstone and Haddon 1996; Buckingham 2002; Lievrouw and Livingstone 2002). For Moores, 'pleasures, like meanings, are the product of a process and can never simply be "read off" from the text' (1990: 25).

What is clear is that during the consumption of a cultural good, a range of levels of engagement are possible and these are structured by a range of factors. Fiske (1992) distinguishes between *semiotic productivity*, whereby the audience engages with the text internally; *enunciative productivity*, whereby they demonstrate externally their engagement with the text; and *textual productivity*, whereby the audience uses the industrially produced text to construct a new text. However, he pays little attention to the institutional or social factors which might shape these productive processes; moreover there is an assumption that all these forms of engagement constitute some form of resistance to the capitalist system. Garnham (2000), quite rightly, calls for a distinction to be made between habitual use, whereby one does something without thinking, and reflexive use, whereby one is critically engaged in the process.

Whatever one's theoretical perspective, studying digital game play challenges us to reconsider theoretical distinctions between producers and consumers and to question our understanding of passive/active media audiences and reception (Fiske and Watts 1985; Fiske 1987; Morley and Silverstone 1990; Ang 1996; Du Gay et al. 1997). Research into the experience of digital game play problematises established terms like 'watching' and 'reading' but also undermines any simplistic understanding of interactivity and play. If the word 'text' is used, it is an expanded concept. And despite the construction of preferred roles and paths, digital games also allow for 'emergent' play (Salen and Zimmerman 2003). Players can transgress the game's rules by cheating or more radically transform the game by modifying it. Both modding communities and cyberartists have produced examples of transgressive and transformative play, thereby expanding our understanding of play itself (Flanagan 2003).

At the same time social, cultural and contextual factors act to constrain these possibilities. Studies of digital game play in arcades, internet cafes, at Local Area Network (LAN) events and in the home provide evidence of the range of factors which intrude into, constrain and facilitate who can play, where, when and how (Schott and Horrell 2000; Newman 2002b; Wright et al. 2002; Bryce and Rutter 2003; Kerr 2003c; Taylor 2003a; Edge 2004b; Nordli 2004). This type of contextualisation of digital play rather dampens the more utopic discussions about the productive and democratic potential of new information and communication technologies (ICTs). Indeed, it challenges the often overstated distinction between virtual and real life and between private and public leisure.

Digital game players have been studied from a variety of perspectives and disciplines. Much of the early work on digital game players was conducted in the psychology field and focused on predicting the effects that digital games had on health and behaviour, particularly in children (Funk 2002). While this work has raised some important issues, the methodological and theoretical weaknesses of this work have been strongly criticised. In many cases little attention was paid to differences between games or to issues of player competence; furthermore the digital game players were usually studied in non-natural environments (Buckingham 2002; Bryce and Rutter 2003). The psychologists were not alone in these deficiencies and early work by media scholars often failed to go beyond the packaging of the games (Skirrow 1986; Provenzo 1991).

In this chapter we shall focus our attention on empirical work that contributes to our understanding of the complex relationship between digital game players, digital games and naturally occurring playing contexts. Given the relative youth of game studies, this work employs a range of disciplinary perspectives and is eclectic in its choice of research methods; ranging from large-scale surveys of digital game players to more micro level studies of gaming practice. In the main the work is small-scale and focused on discrete locations rather than large-scale and comparative, but no doubt in time this situation will be rectified.

This chapter will first examine large-scale surveys of player and non-player demographics. This provides some insights into who plays and how digital game players compare with the producer's implicit and explicit representations of them, as well as why some people play and some do not. The chapter then moves on to examine player preferences and a range of work which explores how digital game players themselves experience digital games and construct cultural practice. The final section of the chapter analyses the influence of context on digital game play.

DIGITAL GAME PLAYERS AND DEMOGRAPHICS

Game consoles are becoming 'mass market', according to one report, because in the USA and Japan over 50 percent of households own one (Spectrum 2002: 13). This trend will accelerate, it is argued, with the introduction of more game platforms. Another report points out that while the USA is the largest market currently, strong growth is expected in the Asia Pacific region including South Korea and China over the next five years (DataMonitor 2002). While household penetration is high in the USA, Japan and Western Europe, there are clearly many markets around the world where digital games are not 'mass market', defined either in terms of the numbers of households who have access to the platforms, or the number of people who play. Even in the USA a recent report noted that household penetration was growing rather slowly and that many households had consoles from previous generations (DFC Intelligence 2004).

Industry surveys give us some insight into who might actually be using these consoles. In 2001 the IDSA (now the ESA), commissioned research which found that nearly 60 percent of American men and women, aged over 18, 'regularly' play digital games. Of these almost 37 percent were aged between 18 and 35 years and 13 percent were over 50 years. The research also found that 43 percent of game players were women and the average age of these women was 29 years. These findings suggest that game playing in 2001 was becoming a widespread leisure activity across all age groups and for both sexes. Another survey of 1,350 homes in 2003 found that game players were continuing to age, with only 38 percent of console game players and only 30 percent of computer game players aged less than 18 years. Meanwhile, while 72 percent of console game players were male, that fell to 58 percent with PC games, indicating an interesting difference in the player demographics of each platform.

While these surveys provide welcome public relations for the games industry, and have been widely cited by academics, they leave many questions unanswered. In the first IDSA survey no explanation was given of terms like 'regularly' or even how many people were surveyed. The surveys also say nothing about duration of play and how this breaks down by demographics (Kline et al. 2003: 266). The reports are also remarkably silent on class and ethnicity.

The Computer Entertainment Software Association (CESA) is the industry trade organisation in Japan. A survey conducted in 2001 in Japan (n=1,013) found that the number of people who 'still play' games has decreased to 27.8 percent, while the numbers who used to play or were 'not willing to play' had increased between 2000 and 2001 (CESA 2002). They also found that twice as many males as females play video games, and females were more likely never to have played or to have played only a couple of times. Of the active game players, 67 percent were males and 33 percent were females, with the highest proportions for both sexes in the 7–12 age group. Across all age groups more males than females played digital games.

CESA categorised their total population into four consumer categories: active, dormant, prospective and disinterested. Disinterested customers were those who had never played and did not want to, or had played and had no intention of playing again. Disinterested customers constituted the largest proportion of those surveyed at 35.8 percent. Dormant customers were players who were waiting for games to be made which would make them want to play again; these constituted

TABLE 5.1   Categorisation of gaming customers in Japan, 2001 and 1999

	Definition	2001 General Public	1999 General Public
Active Game Players	'I play regularly'	27.8%	39.3%
Dormant	'I used to play but now stop playing. I want to try again only if any software interests me'	28.1%	24.3%
Prospective	'I have never tried but I want to try if any software interests me'	8.3%	12.2%
Disinterested	'I have never tried and I won't' and 'I used to play but I won't anymore'	35.8%	24.2%

Source: CESA (2002: 58–62)

28.1 percent. Only 27.8 percent were described as active players, down from almost 40 percent in 1999.

While dormant customers were divided almost evenly between males and females, females constituted a larger proportion of the prospective and disinterested groups. In addition, while the average age of active game players was 23.4, the average age of dormant customers was 31.6 years. Prospective and disinterested players were aged 33.4 and 37.2 years respectively. Clearly the industry has a large potential market of females and people aged above 25 years, which it is not as yet satisfying, at least in Japan. People in the non-active groups explained that they were too busy with work to play games, games were too complicated or games were not fun. In both the USA and Japan game content, perceptions about games, and stage of life seem to influence who plays.

These industry surveys both challenge and reinforce certain stereotypes. While more females and older people are playing digital games than in previous decades, the most frequent game players are males, by a factor of two, and the highest proportion are aged between 7–12 years. The Japanese survey also points to the perceived limitations of current game software and the need for a greater range of software, or certainly different types of software, if dormant and prospective consumers are to be reached. More radical tactics may be needed to reach disinterested consumers.

There have been a small number of academic surveys on digital game players, although many focus on children and teenagers and they are mainly conducted in the USA and Europe (Kline 1998; Roe and Muijs 1998; Wright et al. 2001; Livingstone 2002; Fromme 2003). As with the industry surveys, 'access' to game consoles in the home is high with over 80 percent of households in the USA and just over two-thirds of households in the UK owning a console of some sort. Other European countries display lower percentages for access to game consoles, with Sweden (62 percent), France (57 percent) and Spain (54 percent) the only other European countries reaching above 50 percent (Livingstone 2002). Northern European countries and the USA also have high rates of access to home computers, with the Netherlands leading the way (84 percent), followed by the USA (73 percent), Finland (70 percent) and Sweden (66 percent).

Academic surveys show conflicting evidence as to the correlation between ownership of particular platforms and class, sex and age. A UK study, for example, found that working-class families were more likely to own a games console and middle-class families more likely to own a PC (Livingstone, 2002b: 39). By comparison a German study found no relationship between parents' occupation and ownership of particular platforms (Fromme 2003). In the UK study both age and sex were also significant. Families with young males (6–8 years) were twice as likely to own a game console and families with older males (9–14) were more likely to own a PC (2002: 39).

Of course, owning or having access to a games platform is no indication that the platform is actually used and says nothing about who uses it. One survey of media use in families with children under 12 years (N=2902) in the USA found that only 25 percent had played digital games at least once during the study period (Wright et al. 2001). A survey in British Columbia, Canada, of 11–18 year old children (N=650) found that the average amount of time spent playing was 5 hours per week and that a majority of their sample were only 'sort of interested' (46 percent) or 'not interested at all (37 percent) in playing digital games (Media Analysis Laboratory 1998). Livingstone's study in the UK (2002b: 62) meanwhile found that while digital games were played by two-thirds of 6–17 year olds, use was occasional, averaging less than an hour a day. Indeed, one in five boys and two in five girls never play, despite having access to game platforms.

Few academic studies have been conducted with older age groups. Jones (2003), in a study of American college and university students, found that 70 percent of them reported playing regularly, or occasionally, and that more women than men reported playing computer and online games – 60 percent of women compared to 40 percent of men. Again little explanation is given as to what 'regularly' means. What these surveys show us is that for children, teenagers and young adults, digital game playing is a regular or occasional activity in the USA, Canada and the UK. What they also show is that while many have access to digital games, not everyone plays and for most people the frequency and duration of play are not very high when compared to other media activities.

To put the data about digital game play into context, it is useful to compare levels of play with levels of use of other media. In terms of total number of hours spent per person per annum on different media in the USA, cable and satellite television top the chart with 851 hours, while video games only account for 84 hours. Interestingly, recorded music (228) and daily newspapers (175) scored higher than video games (MPAA 2002). A survey in the UK found that radio and television together absorbed over half of the free time available for media consumption per week, with leisure software/digital games accounting for 1.5 hours a week on average. However, the amount of time spent on leisure software increased from 8 minutes to 81 minutes between 1985 and 2000, which represents a nine-fold increase. The only media to grow more quickly were mobile and online media (Screen Digest 2002). So digital games are clearly absorbing an increasing amount of time for a growing number of people but they absorb less time than traditional broadcast, recorded music and print media.

A small percentage of digital game players spend more time than average playing digital games and are thus defined as 'heavy users' or 'game enthusiasts'. Definitions of 'heavy users' vary and in some cases seem rather low in the first instance. Roe (1998) found that 10 percent of his sample (N = 890) played more than 2 hours a day and these were predominantly male (76.8 percent) and more likely to come from working-class backgrounds. This is supported by Livingstone's work in the UK (2002b: 62). The report by the Media Analysis Laboratory (1998) in British Columbia found that game enthusiasts were more likely to be boys, who tended to play twice as much as girls and were more likely to own more than one console. Griffiths (1997) found a similar significant correlation between sex and both frequency of play and duration of play in a study of almost 150 pre-teenage children in the UK. A slightly later American study found that 10 percent of children play computer games for more than 1 hour a day (Rideout et al. 1999).

These studies suggest that while many people have access to digital game platforms, not all of them play, and of those who play only a small proportion can be called heavy users. Of these heavy users it appears that the majority are male. A number of reasons are offered as to why males, particularly those under 30, are more likely to play more often. The primary reason given is game content. Based on content analysis of games many academics argue that the greater numbers of male players are related to the prevalence of masculine themes of violence and competition in games, the dominance of male avatars and the submissive ways in which female characters are represented (Skirrow 1986; Kinder 1991; Provenzo 1991; Alloway and Gilbert 1998). Even if there are signs that the dominance of male avatars is changing and that there are fewer submissive female characters in games (Jansz and Martis 2003), there are still many games whose themes could be described as masculine. Some representatives of the games industry support this argument and add that the packaging and advertising of games may also alienate many males and females (Laurel 2001; Ray 2004).

More recent academic work argues that content analysis and a focus on representations in games are insufficient to understand the appeal and pleasure which digital games afford. They note that many females play digital games and are able to successfully negotiate, or in some cases modify, the given subject positions (Yates and Littleton 1999; Consalvo 2003b; Kerr 2003b). Indeed, they argue that how characters are represented in a game may be less important that what one can do with them during play and the places and scenarios one encounters – an argument we encountered in Chapter 2. During digital game play the player is not passively identifying with the avatar, as one might do with a lead character in a film, but rather actively playing the avatar (Bryce and Rutter 2002a; Carr 2002; Kennedy 2002; Newman 2002a; Consalvo 2003b). Newman (2002a) states that contemporary 'videogame representation is indicative of an industry in its immaturity still struggling to understand itself' and he vehemently asserts that character capabilities are more important than character representation during game play. Pure content analysis of games must, it is argued, be supplemented by analysis of how players actually interpret, play and in some cases subvert the given themes and avatars if we are to understand gaming as a cultural practice.

Both arguments make important points. Clearly representations in digital games can only be properly understood in the context of the game and game play. Nevertheless, one cannot ignore the role that the language and images used in digital game packaging, marketing and merchandising play in terms of the general public's perception of digital games (Schott and Horrell 2000; CESA 2002; Gansmo et al. 2003; Kerr 2003b). More worryingly, the representations used in some industry packaging and marketing and the findings of content analysis studies may serve to fuel moral panics about digital games and to bolster the case of politicians who support censorship of them (Wark 1994; Lumby 1997; Jenkins 1999; Southern 2001). For this reason, the symbolism and representation of digital games cannot be dismissed lightly.

Another problem that the surveys have highlighted is that being labelled a 'gamer' may have certain social costs attached and these may dissuade people from taking up the subject position of a gamer. Kerr (2003b) found that many females did not classify themselves as 'gamers' given the term's association with hardcore male gamers, who play frequently and who spend considerable sums of money on hardware and software. People who play infrequently, or who play mini games or mobile phone games are called 'casual gamers' by the industry but would not necessarily call themselves 'gamers' at all. There is a clear need to deconstruct and expand the terminology used to describe game players.

DIGITAL GAME PLAYERS: PREFERENCES AND PLEASURES

Player preferences are most commonly expressed in terms of genre. In a consumer survey in 2003, the ESA found that the most frequently played console games were action, followed by driving/racing, sports and role playing. The most frequently played computer games were puzzle, followed by action, driving/racing and sports. Online, people were most likely to play puzzle/trivia, followed by strategy/action/ sports and MMOGs.

Three things stand out in this survey. First, the most frequently played PC and online games (puzzle/trivia games) are not the top-selling genres for those platforms – in fact, most puzzle and trivia games are distributed free. Second, puzzle/trivia games are 'pick-up-and-play' games of relatively short duration and thus they have a shallow learning curve. Third, females were more likely to play PC games (42 percent) and online games (40 percent) than console games (28 percent). These findings challenge both our stereotypes of digital games and of digital game players and it is interesting that most content analyses of games never include puzzle and trivia games in their samples.

Academic studies that investigate game preferences defined by genre provide rather limited and inconclusive insights into demographics. In many studies, boys who played frequently preferred action, fighting and sports games. Girls and boys who played less frequently preferred platform or puzzle games (Griffiths 1997: 230; Kline 1998: 10; Roe and Muijs 1998: 189; Fromme 2003: 9). Gailey (1993) found limited sex and class differences in game preferences. In this study both boys and girls enjoyed 'fantasy-adventure' games and 'spatial' games while only boys played the sports games regularly and only working-class boys played the 'urban-violence' games. Wright et al. (2001) developed their own classification of games and found that only in sports games was there a significant variation by sex. These studies suggest that focusing merely on the genre of games is not sufficient to explain game preferences and demographics.

One of the problems with these studies stems from the fact that game genres, as we saw in Chapter 2, are rather poorly defined. Indeed, many contemporary games are genre hybrids or even post-genre (Nutt and Railton 2003). For example, *GTA: Vice City* (2002) might be categorised as a driving/racing game, as a shoot 'em-up and/or an action/adventure game but this tells us little about the pleasures of playing that particular game. *The Sims* (2000) invented a whole new genre of game. Preferences categorised by game genres may also tell us little, or indeed obfuscate, the range of pleasures and displeasures, which game players find in particular genres.

Second, some of the variations in results can be explained by differences in how the genres are defined. For example, Ray (2004) found that in general junior high school girls did not like fighting games. However, further discussions revealed that what the girls disliked was fighting against the same opponents over and over again, not fighting per se. In general they favoured indirect competition and team play over direct competition. Thus surveys of game preferences categorised by genre operate at too general a level to offer us real insights into the pleasures and displeasures of digital games and how these vary by demographics.

Qualitative studies of game players usefully supplement player surveys by providing more insight into the nature and range of player pleasures and displeasures. While pleasure is a term which is defined differently in different disciplines, and has a particular association within media studies with psychoanalytic approaches to media texts and with studies of gender and media use (O'Connor and Klaus 2000), in this section I shall use the term as a heuristic to explore the factors that increase or decrease pleasurable game play experiences (Kerr et al. 2006).

Interviews and focus groups with female players have found that while they play a broad range of game genres, they tend to prefer those that afford the player some degree of 'freedom'. Freedom in this context can refer to a variety of things, ranging from the freedom to explore the gameworld without necessarily completing particular missions, to the freedom to create or play a variety of characters (Yates and Littleton 1999; Schott and Horrell 2000; Kerr 2003). These types of freedoms are usually discussed in the literature in terms of degrees of control and agency (Aarseth 1997; Murray 1997). Control is a fundamental aspect of different modes of play according to the early game theorists. For Roger Caillois, agôn, or competitive play, is a struggle for control between two players. Games of chance can be seen as relinquishing control to dice or cards, while performative play (mimicry) relates to the pleasures of adopting another identity and losing control of one's own (Caillois 2001).

Digital games vary in the degree of freedom or control they allow the player and in the degree to which they can adapt to the player's style – and this struggle for control between the player and the game generates a range of unique experiences. Aarseth (1997) distinguishes between games that a player can manipulate, which he calls 'dynamic' games, and games that the player cannot manipulate, which he calls 'static' games. Newman (2003) argues that many games are full of breaks and intermissions and that during gameplay a player is engaged to varying degrees. He conceptualises these degrees of engagement along a continuum between what he calls online and offline states. For Newman, games restrict the player's exploratory and navigational freedom in certain places in order to foreground particular types of gameplay. The imposition of such limitations is interesting to consider, given the varying preferences for manipulability expressed in studies of digital game players. In addition, player preference for freedom and flexibility may be culturally specific. Recent research has found that the degree of freedom offered by games like *GTA: Vice City* (2002), while important to Western game players, was less

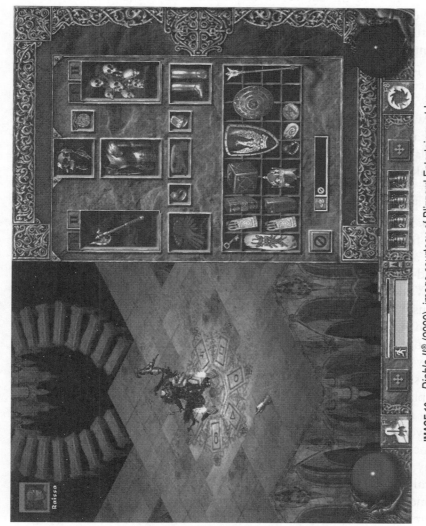

IMAGE 10 *Diablo II*® (2000), image courtesy of Blizzard Entertainment Inc.

important to their Japanese counterparts (Joyner and TerKeurst 2003; Edge 2004).

Studies of particular games within genres give us some insight into the multiplicity of pleasures generated, although they are often quite mute on the subject of displeasure. Taylor (2003a) found that players of *EverQuest* (1999), an MMOG, highlighted the pleasures of mastery and of exploration, identity and team play, social interaction/community as well as combat. Schott and Horrell (2000) also identified the pleasure of exploration in RPGs. Exploration and the mastery of space are important themes in the games theory literature (Friedman 1995; Fuller and Jenkins 1995; Aarseth 1997; Manovich 2001). Both Newman (2003) and Ryan (2001) situate the debate within the wider literature on 'cyberspace' and virtual reality. Jenkins points to the replacement of real world place spaces with 'safe' virtual play spaces (Jenkins, cited in Buckingham 2002). Similarly, different games offer different 'spatial typologies' as Newman (2003: 115) calls them. We can begin to think about what this means by analysing and comparing *Prince of Persia: The Sands of Time* (2003) to *The Sims 2* (2004). In the former the player usually has a third-person perspective and views the action from behind the main avatar. In the latter the player has a 'god-like' perspective and views the main characters from above.

While many players will never experience all of the levels and diversions within a game, it is clear that as a player's competence and knowledge of a game world increases, the nature of his/her pleasures may also change. Taylor (2003a) found that female game players enjoyed the power they felt when they succeeded in battles in *EverQuest* and she links this to the pleasure of game mastery. She also identified a category of players in *EverQuest* whom she called 'power gamers', who played in a manner which many people would not consider as fun or leisure. Power gamers in her study were committed to fully understanding the structure of a game and tended to focus on efficiency and instrumental play, on setting and achieving goals and displayed high levels of technical and skill proficiency (Taylor 2003b). While in some cases power gamers played the same number of hours as casual gamers, their results were often much more successful in terms of their character's progress and social standing in the game world.

Early studies of the internet asserted that 'trying on' or 'performing' alternative identities was one of the key pleasures (Turkle 1997). Similarly, some studies of digital games note that they offer people a chance to perform alternative or socially prohibited identities and fantasies, or indeed to hide one's own (Kennedy 2002; Consalvo 2003; Filiciak 2003; Taylor 2003a). In some cases this is an intertextual pleasure and linked to the performance of characters from other media texts like James Bond, Harry Potter or Legolas. For Buckingham (2002) and Kendall (2002) identity play in digital games may merely reflect the complexity of identity in post-modern societies. However, the player's ability to negotiate representations and subject positions may be strongly influenced by other factors, including competence and age (Green et al. 1998).

The potential for identity play, or what Caillois (2001) would call mimicry, varies from game to game and platform to platform. Empirical studies point to some female game players being quite critical of the imagery and limited range of identities offered by console games and the player's need to negotiate the given subject positions (Yates and Littleton 1999; Schott and Horrell 2000; Kennedy 2002; Kerr 2003b). MMOGs may allow a player to create more than one avatar per server and while identity play is clearly an important aspect of the pleasures offered by this genre, female games players may still struggle with, or 'bracket', the given representations (Taylor 2003a). PC games like *The Sims* (2000) offer a range of character possibilities and the control afforded the player in this regard may account, in part, for its popularity with female game players (Nutt and Railton 2003). By comparison racing games and puzzle games may offer limited opportunities for identity play.

As mentioned in the previous section, there is some disagreement in the games literature as to the importance of the visual representation of one's character in a game. Some studies argue that the underlying characteristics or capabilities of an avatar are more important than its visual representation and situate identity play more in terms of the varying situations one encounters in a game (Kinder 1991; Kennedy 2002; Newman 2002a, 2003). Thus one may need a fast, less powerful avatar in some situations and a stronger, slower avatar in others. Indeed, according to Jenkins, game characters can be seen to operate in two distinct spheres: (i) as characters in non-interactive game sequences like cut-scenes and on game packaging, and (ii) as avatars, where their function in the game supersedes their representation and they become a vehicle which the player deploys within the game world (Jenkins, cited in Buckingham 2002). Newman (2003) argues that game characters/avatars are purposely devoid of personality so that the player can embody them and exploit their functionality. Further, he argues that as a player's experience grows, their selection of game characters will be influenced more by their capabilities and less by their representation. Clearly these ideas require further exploration before we can reconcile the role of game characters within a game and their role outside of it, in terms of fan culture, advertising and marketing. Further, the extent to which players personalise their characters and appearance in multiplayer games, particularly MMOGs, may signal that visual representation is of greater importance in these types of games.

Researchers have also identified social interaction and community as key pleasures of digital games. While sociality may be thought of as a feminine pleasure, and as such is more associated with female game players, the growth of online game play in all genres has confounded such simplistic assumptions. Social interaction and community in digital games, as Taylor (2003a) points out, can be multi-layered with both in-game (e.g. chat and bulletin boards) and out-of-game aspects (e.g. swapping games, talking about strategies and cheats) (McFarlane et al. 2002; Buckingham and Sefton-Green 2003). Wright et al. (2002) documents the extent of in-game social interaction between male players of *Counter-Strike,* ranging from creative verbal dialogue during game play to the design of non-verbal (e.g. logos, avatars, modified maps) expressions. Newman (2003), Schott and Kambouri (2003), Ermi and Mäyrä (2003), Klastrup (2003) and Nordli (2004) amongst others, have explored extra-diegetic or out-of-game social interaction and noted how digital game play is frequently shared by people who are not directly interacting with the game but who are actively engaged. Newman calls these 'secondary players'. We will return to out-of-game social interaction in the next section.

Sociality may be more culturally specific than gender specific. One study of variations in game preferences between countries, specifically the UK and Japan, found that social aspects of gaming were very important to teenage Japanese game players and strongly constrain their genre and game selection, while competition was more important to UK teenagers (Joyner and TerKeurst 2003; Edge 2004b). Observations of Japanese teenagers and British teenagers playing the same racing game found remarkable differences in playing style, with the Japanese teenagers slowing down at the finish line so they could cross the line alongside their competitor. Such findings indicate that regardless of how competition is structured within a game, during game play players may develop their own style and strategies.

Marshall notes that 'the pleasure of the game is that the rules are made and remade, transformed and shifted by the players' (2002: 80). For some, a key pleasure is not playing by the rules of the game but finding ways to transform or subvert the rules – a pleasure which is linked to the pleasure of control and performance but may, in some instances, reduce the pleasure of play for others, particularly in MMOGs. While adjusting the rules of a game can be part of the pre-game negotiations in both non-digital and digital games, changing the rules of the game to improve one's chances of success without informing the other players is not. Kücklich (2004) notes that cheats range from those which affect the game-space, to those which adjust game-time or enhance player agency.

For example, some cheats, like walkthroughs, merely help one to overcome obstacles and puzzles, while the use of 'aimbots' in FPS or 'duping' in MMOGs allows a player to greatly enhance his/her chances of winning. Thus the consequences of cheats for players vary but they are particularly an issue in MMOGs, where many people play together and detecting cheating is much more difficult. Cheating in MMOGs and cheats that modify hardware so players can play imported games are actively discouraged by game companies and they exert a lot of time and money to try and control these efforts. Cheats in single player games are by comparison actively encouraged by the industry, who benefit from the sales of books, magazines and premium helplines which offer solutions, walkthroughs and short-cut codes. Players themselves may benefit from cheating in extra-diegetic ways also. In one Irish study a particularly resourceful teenager offered a consultancy cheat service to his classmates whereby he would source relevant cheats online for people for a fee (Kerr et al. 2004).

Game companies often support other forms of 'transformative' or 'creative' play. Many PC games are sold with level editors as standard and there is also a wide variety of shareware and freeware, which make altering a digital game, particularly a PC game, less difficult than one might suspect. Within the game-playing community, 'mods' is short for 'modify' or 'modification' and usually refers to 'gamer-made alterations to a commercially available game' (Søtamaa 2004: 2). While clearly not all game players engage in this activity, the productive capacity of some game players and the extent to which these mods circulate across the internet demonstrate the degree to which what Fiske calls a 'shadow cultural economy' operates in this context and how productive such consumption can be (Morris 2003). While the

IMAGE 11   Gordon and Alyx, *Half Life 2* (2001), image provided courtesy of Valve.

actual sale of such productions may be frowned upon by many game players, there have been instances where players have sold their characters and levels online. Indeed, *Counter-Strike* (2000) was a team play modification of an existing commercial game *Half-Life* (1998) and demonstrates that modifications can become full-blown commercial products.

From the release of *Doom* (1993), development companies like id Software, Epic Games and Rockstar have actively encouraged the production of modifications for their games and run elaborate websites and competitions to both encourage and showcase player-made work (Kushner 2003). Further, many companies also look for evidence of modding experience when they are hiring staff and mine community websites for feedback on their products. Some companies release early versions of their games via the internet to allow game players to play test and de-bug them. Despite such active encouragement of productive consumption, publishers have more recently begun to assert their intellectual property rights and End User Licence Agreements (EULAs) may now state that making mods for commercial exploitation is prohibited (Consalvo 2003a; Mactavish 2003; Søtamaa 2004).

Some mods are clearly an attempt by game players to take a global product and make it into something local. This is particularly evident in the replacement of levels with local environments and the replacement of characters with more culturally proxemic representations. However, studies of modders have found that they are motivated more by a desire to demonstrate their computer skills and gain prestige in the modding community (similar in many ways to hackers) than by any broader attempt to resist cultural globalisation (Søtamaa 2004). In other words, it can be hard to find critical reflection and political activism in some of these activities (Garnham 2000). Jenkins (2002) argues that 'the interactive audience is more than a marketing concept and less than "semiotic democracy"'.

At the same time, the circulation of player-created games and patches after September 11th, 2001 indicates that in certain circumstances this political potential is realised. In many cases these are produced by a small, but increasing number of artists who are taking advantage of freeware and shareware to make politically motivated, and resistant, art pieces using commercial games. These interventions can range from the insertion of game patches into games to the development of entire games which question gaming conventions, genres and ideologies. The development of *September 12, Madrid* and *Kabul Kaboom* by developers (see www.newsgaming.com) provides some arresting examples of mini games with strong political messages. Smaller interventions like *Tiny Signs of Hope,* a range of downloadable anti-war

IMAGE 12 *The Sims 2* (2004), image provided courtesy of Electronic Arts.

posters designed for *The Sims* and *Velvet-Strike*, interventionist anti-war graffiti designed to be inserted into *Counter-Strike*, are further examples (Poremba 2003; see also www.opensorcery.net/velvet-strike/sprays.html).

Interventions by female artists address political and gender issues as well as the construction of games themselves. Examples of this work range from inserting modified female images into existing games to making entirely new games on topics which rarely make it into the commercial space: for example, identity, memory and truth (Schleiner 2001; Holmes 2002; Flanagan 2003). Many of these works use irony as a strategy of resistance and to explore male/female subjectivities and passive/active dichotomies. Particular foci are the exploration of 'control' in computer games as it relates to avatars and actions, 'exploration' itself in computer games as it relates to self-discovery, rather than conquest, and to contest the legacy of the military-industrial complex from which digital games emerged. For Flanagan (2003: 379), 'the approach that women digital artists are employing in their work offers an essential counterpoint to digital culture; artists are making cyberculture, a distant and masculine terrain, into an area for more personal exploration.'

While modding, cheating and artistic interventions are part of the wider game culture and provide interesting examples of player creativity and agency, it might be unwise to overstate their prevalence. For many game players game playing is a 'private' activity which takes place in the home with friends and family, or alone when there is nothing better to do (Kerr 2003b; Kerr et al. 2004). Many are content to keep trying until they succeed in overcoming an obstacle or to ask friends for advice rather than buying strategy guides or going online to look for hints. Social networks and peers may be as important a resource for cheats as commercially available options.

User creativity or productivity in more traditional audience studies refers to a range of activities from semiotic and enunciative to textual, as defined earlier in this chapter (Fiske 1992). These forms of productivity can also be found in game culture, although less attention is paid to textual productivity and player-created texts (which build upon, but exist outside, the game) than is given to mods, cheats and artistic interventions (which are placed within the game). For example, some games provide easy to use tools to encourage players to record their play and then to publicly circulate it to other players. *The Sims 2* (2004) allows players to create their own in-game photo albums and '*Sim* films', or mini-videos of one's play. On *The Sims 2* official website one can download official *Sims* endings and music for one's films. This encouragement of fan production by companies is designed to extend a player's relationship with the game and to build game communities. Thus game players are encouraged to circulate their productions or 'meta-texts' on the official game websites. These officially sanctioned productions often exist alongside a range of unofficial sites where players have taken it upon themselves to create their own websites (Nutt and Railton 2003). However, even these unofficial sites have become subject to corporate scrutiny and in some cases other forms of action; the banning of *EverQuest* user Mystere for posting a piece of fanfiction on an unofficial site is just one example (Taylor 2002).

Thus, while game development companies and publishers may construct and represent digital game players and play in certain ways, for example targeting hardcore players of particular genres, players as consumers may occupy the given subject positions and play by the rules, or may actively negotiate, bracket or subvert them. For some digital players it may be pleasurable to play exactly according to the given script, while for others it may be more pleasurable to subvert and transform the script. Qualitative studies of digital game players suggest that the pleasures of digital game play are heterogeneous and vary not only between game segments but also between individual games within these segments. Further, as players gain experience and competence, their pleasures evolve and thus game pleasures can only be understood by studying the relationship between the player, the game and other players in particular contexts.

PLAY CONTEXTS

Digital game play may occur in a variety of contexts and there is a growing body of work which uses surveys, interviews and participant observation to explore the complex interplay of player, game and context. Broadly these explore public spaces where gaming occurs (arcades, internet cafes, bars, universities, public transport and in work), private spaces such as the home, and virtual online spaces as sites of game play (Fiske and Watts 1985; Haddon 1993; Yates and Littleton 1999; Schott and Horrell 2000; Bryce and Rutter 2002a; Newman 2002a, 2002b; Stewart and Choi Park 2002; Wright et al. 2002; Wright and Briedenbach 2002; Jones 2003; Kerr 2003b; Taylor 2003a).

This work gives us an important insight into the diversity of digital game practices and contexts. It also highlights the complex range of factors which influence the enrolment, socialisation and practice of digital game play in different contexts. Some of these factors operate as 'constraints', which have been defined as 'anything that inhibits people's ability to participate in leisure activities' and may serve to 'exclude' certain groups from participating (Bryce and Rutter 2003). For example, Livingstone (2002) notes that children's playing patterns in the home may be heavily influenced by cultural constructions, parental permission and values, the physical and symbolic location of the machines, and lifestyle expectations. Other factors may operate as 'facilitators' and assist in someone's enrolment and socialisation. Yates and Littleton (1999) argue strongly that playing digital games is a socially constructed activity and can only be understood by exploring the practices that game players define as gaming and the language that they use.

Playing a digital game has been described as stepping into a 'magic circle', whereby one agrees to play according to the rules and becomes a willing participant in the game. Studies of how digital game players enter these magic circles highlight the role of friends, family and partners as important facilitators who may enlist people into the games culture. Studies of female game players have found that the key facilitator is usually male and that initially boys and girls may play the same games (Schott and Horrell 2000; Kerr 2003b). During teenage and college years a social network, or what Wright and Briedenbach (2002) call 'friendship networks', who play and provide access to platforms, games and support or advice, are important in terms of maintaining gaming as a leisure activity. For female game players this network tends to be male dominated.

Social relationships may also be important in terms of understanding game preferences, duration and frequency of play. While industrial and academic surveys of ownership of digital game consoles and PCs in the home point to a high level of access – more in-depth studies have found that the owner of the console/PC will often determine who has access and the types of games played. Those with what Schott and Horrell (2000) call 'secondary access' may have less control over what is played and when. In families with children, parental control may constrain both duration of play and game choice but studies have found that children may circumvent these constraints by playing in friends' houses, playing in their bedrooms and by swapping games

(Ermi and Mäyrä 2003; Kerr 2003b). In many households there is a clear 'generation gap' between parents and their children when it comes to knowledge about digital games.

A number of studies have found that female game players are 'contextually restricted' and tend to play games in the home rather than in public game spaces (Schott and Horrell 2000; Bryce and Rutter 2003; Kerr 2003b). Studies conducted in game arcades found that males predominated (Haddon 1988, 1993; Griffiths 1991; Alloway and Gilbert 1998) and the pattern seems to have continued in internet cafes and large LAN parties (Nordli 2004). While the sheer predominance of males in these spaces may act as a constraint for female game players, another factor is that many females may be unwilling to compete publicly against strangers (Griffiths 1991; Kerr 2003b). This may point not to a dislike of competition, but rather to an interesting variation between competing against oneself and friends and competing against strangers. Another constraint may be the in-game discourse. Wright and Briedenbach (2002: 15) found that players often engaged in 'trash talk' or 'the utterance of violent/obscene words that are sexist and homophobic in the extreme, and on rare occasions racist' whilst playing first-person shooters (FPS) online. While many game players take little notice of such talk during game play, some, especially newbies, may find it intimidating. Many female game players take part in female-only competitions which provide a safe environment in which they can compete and practise their skills (Goodwin 2001; Kerr 2003b).

Game playing in internet cafes and LAN parties is seen by game players as a way to socialise and to play co-operative games (Griffiths 1991; Stewart and Choi Park 2002; Wright and Briedenbach 2002; Swalwell 2003; Nordli 2004). A study of a LAN party in Australia found people involved in online play but also offline chat, spectating, negotiation of strategies, repairing and rebuilding computers, viewing machinima, ordering in pizza and drinks (Swalwell 2003). A study of a Norwegian LAN party found that socialising was an important aspect of the experience and participants only played between 3 and 4 hours a day (Nordli 2004). Korean and Japanese studies of PC bangs, their equivalent of internet cafes, and arcades found that they were important social spaces where teenagers could escape from the responsibilities of school, home and work (Yoon 2000; Stewart and Choi

Park 2002; Edge 2004b). In Canada, Wright and Briedenbach (2002) found that multiplayer games on college campuses were an important way to make and maintain friends. The study revealed that games took place in a range of spaces from university dorms to computer laboratories. These studies challenge many of the anti-social stereotypes about digital games and highlight the importance of the offline context to online activities.

Single-player console game play can be social also. Schott and Kambouri (2003) and Green et al. (1998) document a form of collaborative play involving young viewers giving advice and avidly watching the player of a single-player console adventure in domestic settings. Kerr (2003b) found that over-18 game players in multi-tenant houses engaged in 'pad-passing' and collaborative forms of play when playing single-player console games and engaged in lively verbal interaction when playing networked LAN games. Newman (2002a, 2002b, 2003) describes these game spectators as 'co-pilots' and suggests that they are an important part of digital game play. For him digital game play is not always 'ergodic' but should be thought of as encompassing a range of states from 'online' to 'offline', from interactive to detached. Newman maintains that interactivity is not synonymous with digital game play, given that during play one may be distracted, detached or spectating.

While context or the physical location of the game play is clearly important to the experience of digital play, Wright and Briedenbach (2002) suggest that one's engagement with digital games is influenced by the interaction of physical space with two other game spaces. *Game-play space* refers to whether the game is single player, played over a LAN or played using the internet, and whether the game is a death match or team play. *Social-symbolic space* refers to the virtual space where social interactions are produced. Taylor, like Newman, points to the diversity of these social symbolic spaces and argues that the specificities of engagement in MMOGs differ from server to server and depend on the setting one is experiencing within the game. It may also vary depending on whether one is playing with friends, acquaintances or strangers. Indeed, playing digital games online in the home provides important insights into how public and private leisure spaces intersect and overlap in contemporary society and how players can overcome temporal and spatial boundaries in digital game play.

SUMMARY

Digital game play should be seen as a socially constructed, dynamic and diverse cultural practice involving a range of human and non-human actors including producers, publishers, retailers, internet cafes, gaming clubs, technologies, games and users, to name but a few. Within this process not all users have the same power to participate in digital game play and the literature is particularly useful for its analyses of how social factors (e.g. age, gender, race, income and class) operate to 'constrain' digital game players (Fiske and Watts 1985; Fiske 1987; Haddon 1993; Ang 1996; Yates and Littleton 1999; Garnham 2000; Bryce and Rutter 2003). In many cases gaming cannot be separated from the context of play and existing social relationships. This type of research challenges researchers to think beyond broad generic categories and limited player types. It also challenges game designers to think about how to accommodate a range of playing styles, which in turn may help to broaden player demographics.

SIX

NON-ENTERTAINMENT USES OF DIGITAL GAMES

OVERVIEW

Our previous examination of digital games as texts, as cultural industry and as cultural practice may have given the impression that digital games are only used for entertainment and leisure. While most digital games are certainly designed to entertain, and that is where the bulk of the industry's revenue derives, increasingly digital games are being used as learning tools in formal education, industrial training and informal contexts. The education supplement of the *Guardian* newspaper in the UK on one day carried two stories about the potential of digital games in formal educational contexts: 'Let the games begin' and 'Welcome to play school' (Dodson 2004; McClean 2004). Governments also have a role to play in this development and there are examples in many countries of policies that promote the pedagogic and cultural potential of ICTs, and within this digital games, in both formal and informal contexts. Thus, while the digital games industry and culture certainly circulate globally, one cannot ignore the interventions of a range of international, national and local public bodies who are actively promoting, regulating and struggling to define digital games as cultural practice in local contexts.

In this chapter we shall briefly examine different learning theories before focusing on the design and use of digital games in formal, industrial and information learning contexts. These initiatives will be situated within broader attempts by governments in some countries to promote the use of ICTs in the context of lifelong learning. Finally, we shall explore the implications which non-entertainment uses of digital games have for our understanding of games and violence.

DIGITAL GAMES AND LEARNING THEORIES

There is broad agreement amongst academics and policy-makers that digital games are highly motivating and engaging for game players. Similarly, it is generally acknowledged that players must assimilate a lot of information in order to progress in a game and that they engage, to some degree, in a form of learning in order to work out the best strategies in order to win. However, there is disagreement as to the type of learning which occurs during digital game play and the degree to which this type of learning can be transferred or replicated in non-entertainment games and in formal learning contexts.

Marc Prensky has proposed that digital games can encourage learning in new ways which challenge accepted conventions and practices in schools. The following list from Prensky (2001) compares learning with digital games to conventional school and lecture-based learning:

- Twitch speed versus conventional speed
- Parallel processing versus linear processing
- Text illustrating the image rather than vice versa
- Random access versus step by step
- Connectivity: synchronous and asynchronous electronic information and communication versus standalone
- Active versus passive: communicating and participating as well as reading
- Orientation towards problem solving: play versus work
- Immediate reward: payoff versus patience
- Fantasy versus reality
- A positive view of technology, brought about by its presence everywhere, unlike previous generations.

James Paul Gee (2003) argues that digital game players engage in what he calls 'critical learning' while playing certain games. He contends that the type of learning required by digital games is 'close to what I believe are the best theories of learning in cognitive sciences' (2003: 1–12). Gee distinguishes between passive learning, active learning and critical learning: He argues that in good games (and for him not all games are good), players consciously engage in *critical learning*, which involves evaluating, reflecting and manipulating the design grammar (2003: 40). In particular, he highlights the fact that games empower learners, facilitate problem solving in various ways, and facilitate a more realistic understanding of how things work (Gee 2004). For him digital games have the potential to encourage the development of critical thinking skills which can be applied in other contexts. Moreover he believes that the type of learning one may do in good games surpasses a lot of the more passive forms of learning which take place in formal environments like schools (Gee 2003: 46).

Gee is very enthusiastic about the type of learning which digital games can foster. As a (former) cognitive scientist, he sees playing digital games as a way of exercising one's learning muscle, of developing one's innate desire for learning, and as an important precursor domain which develops learning and thinking styles of use in other domains such as science and computers (2003: 48). It is a viewpoint that is not shared by everyone. Others would argue that the critical learning skills acquired while playing digital games do not necessarily transfer into other contexts and that learning in/with digital games is not necessarily educationally worthwhile (Davenport 2002; Buckingham and Sefton-Green 2003: 391). Buckingham, an educationalist, clearly believes that learning involves more than a cognitive or mental process and he is critical of theories that view knowledge, skills and learning in a decontextualised manner. While he agrees with Gee that learning how to learn is important, he argues that there is more to learning than the individual and the technology. (See http://labweb.education.wisc.edu/room130 and www.londonknowledge lab.ac.uk for more information on the work of these two academics.)

A recent report published by the Department of Education and Skills in the UK (Kirriemuir and McFarlane 2004) may help us to place the Gee and Buckingham arguments in context. This report identifies four different theories of learning (the behaviourist, the cognitive, the humanist and the social/situational), and lists what each theory views as the site of learning and the role of education in the learning process:

- *The behaviourist approach* views learning in terms of behavioural change and argues that this takes place when adequate external resources and tasks are provided. Education can provide these resources and tasks.
- *The cognitive approach* views learning as something that takes place inside one's head and so making connections in one's head is the site of learning. In this approach, education can develop the capacity and skills for one to learn better.

- *The humanist approach* is about the development of a person's potential and involves emotional and attitudinal development. In this approach, education tries to make a person more self-reliant and autonomous.
- *The social and situational approach* views learning as something that takes place in a group context and is dependent upon the relationship between people and the learning environment. Education in this approach provides the opportunity to participate in communities of practice.

While these different approaches are not necessarily mutually exclusive, they do help us to understand how different authors can view the potential of digital games quite differently. Gee takes a cognitive approach to learning while Buckingham takes a social/situational approach with some insights from the humanist approach.

DIGITAL GAMES AND LEARNING IN DIFFERENT CONTEXTS

FORMAL EDUCATIONAL CONTEXTS

Social and situational factors were important influences on digital game play in the last chapter and I believe are no less so in formal educational contexts. An evaluation of the usefulness of commercial off-the-shelf games in both primary and secondary schools in the UK identified three ways in which digital games can be used to support learning: (i) learning as a result of tasks stimulated by the content of the game (ii) knowledge developed through the content of the game, and (iii) skills arising as a result of playing the game (McFarlane et al. 2002). However, the report goes on to argue that these benefits can be reduced if there is a mismatch between game content and curriculum content and if the type of skills which digital game play encourages are not explicitly valued by assessment criteria. The report also identified a number of areas where commercial games could be altered to address the formal educational context: by allowing the player to save and store scores; by offering non-identical repeats; by allowing a player to save and restart at the same place; by tailoring play to class lengths and class timetables; by ensuring that the content is accurate; by providing a manual for teachers; and by ensuring that the reading age of the player is matched to the text (2002: 29–31).

These arguments are supported by work elsewhere. Kurt Squire (in press: 10) argues that we need to distinguish between learning from, and learning with, a game. For him a game like *Civilization III* (2001) is a useful learning tool and offers not only a more geographic materialist perspective on history than the traditional approach to history teaching but also a sense of the interconnections between countries and people at different time periods. In a study of how *Civilization III* was used in one urban city school in the USA, Squire and Barab (2004) found that the game had motivational value once the students could connect it with personal goals and interests. In this particular study the largely African-American students used the game to explore and replay colonial history. However, the students also found *Civilization III* rather complex and sometimes frustrating and uninteresting; indeed, the paper is rather critical of those who believe that all students will find games interesting. Consequently, the value of commercial off-the-shelf games, they argue, is that they challenge ingrained ways of thinking about learning and teaching.

A similar perspective is developed by Egenfeldt-Nielsen (2004). Following his study of the use of *Europa Universalis II* (2001) over a period of 7 weeks with a class of 86 students aged 15–17 years in Denmark, he argues that digital games offer a dynamic and rich presentation mode. However, he is realistic about the range of barriers faced by schools who wish to use commercial off-the-shelf games. In his study, he identified 10 potential barriers to the use of commercial games in current educational settings, including: classroom time schedule; physical set-up of the classroom; class expectations; teacher background; genre knowledge; technical problems; experience with group work; need for teacher preparation; perception of games; and class size. He also underscores the need to balance game and learning dynamics and notes that in short-term projects like his, game dynamics can dominate.

Research aimed at exploring the potential of commercial off-the-shelf games in formal education contexts is partially motivated by what are seen as the weaknesses of current educational software. Many argue that current e-learning software companies have not been very successful in balancing the game and fun-like elements of their products with their educational and learning objectives. Further, it is argued that both e-learning and games companies do not seem to understand the constraints of time, resources, curriculum and examinations that teachers, parents and students work under (Kirriemuir and McFarlane 2004). Despite these arguments the formal education

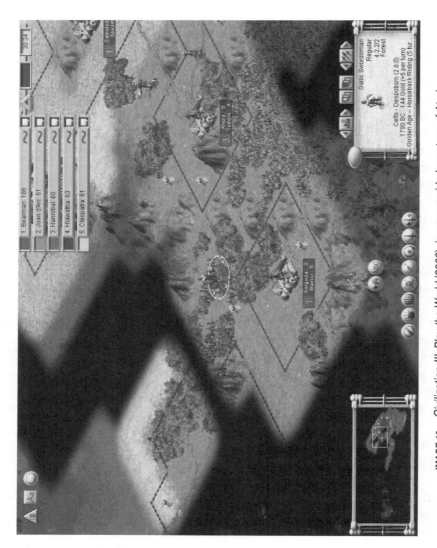

IMAGE 13 *Civilization III: Play the World* (2002), image provided courtesy of Atari.

sector does not seem to offer sufficient financial incentives to either e-learning companies or digital games companies to encourage them to design educational software with these constraints in mind.

A recent research report on the priorities for future European research programmes (Behrendt et al. 2003) argued that the Commission 'can play an important role in fostering educational innovations' and went on to argue that future research programmes should fund basic research and game based e-learning prototypes, since the private sector did not seem in a position to do this. At present the European Commission funds a number of educational research projects, including the m-learning project, which looks at mobile learning applications, and the Kaleidoscope network, involving 800 researchers and 76 research centres working on technology enhanced learning (see www.kaleidoscope.imag.fr and www.m-learning.org). At the same time, Behrendt et al. argue that the low level of integration of ICT in Europe's classrooms means that 'if all networked computers were to disappear tomorrow, Europe's classrooms would be one of the least affected areas of society' (2003: 12). Indeed it is evident from this report that the uneven distribution of ICT resources across different types of schools and across countries remains probably the most significant constraint on the use of games in formal educational contexts.

It might be expected that the third-level sector would have fewer curriculum and examination constraints than primary and secondary level. An overview of this sector finds the use of simulations and games in a variety of subject areas and for both pedagogic and research purposes. In the USA the Massachusetts Institute of Technology (MIT) has been a pioneer in terms of both proponents and projects dealing with ICTs in education, from Seymour Papert's enthusiastic writings about children, computers and learning in the early 1980s, to MIT Media Lab's Toys of Tomorrow (1997) project. The Comparative Media Program at MIT and the Learning Sciences and Technology Lab at Microsoft also collaborated on the Games-to-Teach project, which sought to raise awareness of the pedagogical potential of games by developing conceptual frameworks to offer guidance on how games might be used to teach maths, science and engineering at secondary and undergraduate level (Holland et al. 2003). This project has spawned the Education Arcade consortium, which plans to develop some of the Games-to-Teach conceptual frameworks into game prototypes.

Another project at MIT is focusing on the use of simulations and games for teaching at third level. Professor John Belcher has been involved in the Studio Physics project, whereby undergraduate physics lectures were combined with 3D visualisations and hands-on experiments using computers. The aim of Studio Physics was to see if the introduction of ICT-based teaching and learning tools might address attendance and failure rates in introductory physics courses. Similarly, in the University of Auckland, New Zealand, research into collaborative virtual environments for education and research have experimented with the *Half-Life* and *Torque* game engines as tools for visualising architectural design. These types of 'blended learning' solutions, which mix virtual and physical teaching methods to varying degrees, appear to achieve good motivational results, although the learning and knowledge outputs remain less clear at this stage. Similar projects can be found at Anglia Polytechnic University's Ultralab, NESTA's (the National Endowment for Science, Technology and the Arts) Futurelab, and the London Knowledge Lab in the UK. Digital games are also used in the teaching of humanities subjects in third-level institutions. Janet Murray (1997) describes a class in MIT on the 'Structure and Interpretation of Nonlinear and Interactive Narrative', in which the fictional structure of certain digital games are used as examples of interactive fiction.

Wolf provides us with a history of the study of video games and notes that 'at the turn of the millennium, video game theory, as a field of study, included a handful of books, several academic conferences, the first online academic journal (*Game Studies*), and over half a dozen annual conferences' (Wolf and Perron 2003: 2–13). Things have changed very rapidly. A 2001 report noted that there were 22 third-level institutions in the UK offering game-specific courses, ranging from game programming, animation and design to game studies and theory (DTI 2001). From 2004 the A-level media studies course in the UK also offers an option to study digital games.

It is clear that some private companies, public education bodies and academic research groups have been examining the potential role of a range of information and communications technologies (ICTs), including digital games, in schools. The evidence so far suggests that games can prove useful in terms of motivation to learn and can facilitate collaborative learning and communication skills. Simulations have proven useful as a cheap alternative to expensive equipment and in relation to the visualization of complex concepts and ideas. However, neither games nor simulations are cost free and clear barriers remain to using commercial off-the-shelf games in education. These barriers include: the training and role of the teacher/lecturer, the content and diversity of commercial games and their relevance to curricula and examinations, negative attitudes/perceptions towards games and finally very real technical and cost issues (McFarlane et al. 2002; Kirriemuir and McFarlane 2004). Thus while one can argue that digital games have the potential to stimulate a more progressive pedagogy, it will require the enrolment of multiple stakeholders and the deployment of significant resources to equip and train educational institutions to exploit this potential.

DIGITAL GAMES AND LEARNING IN INDUSTRY

Both non-digital and digital games are well-established tools for management, corporate training and recruitment. The Serious Games Initiative in the USA has highlighted their role with regard to public and private policy, health and more generally in management and training (see www.seriousgames.org). In these contexts the safe and relatively cheap simulation of both everyday work situations and future scenarios have employed role play and exploited the visualisation, communicative and collaborative potential of games. Games have also been used to assess personality types and develop training programmes within companies. However, of all the industries that use digital games, the military is arguably one of the most extensive users.

Game theorists like Huizinga and Caillois have both examined the history and relationship between war and games (Huizinga 1949; Caillois 2001). In Chapter 2 we recounted some early links between the digital games industry and the military – pointing out, for example, that Sanders Associates, who manufactured the first videogame console for the home, was a military electronics firm. Kline et al. (2003) give a more detailed account of the 'military derivation' of digital games and the use of simulations and virtual reality technologies in contemporary military planning as well as military training (2003: 179–83).

Examples of the relationship between the military and the digital games industry abound. In the 1980s Atari was commissioned by the American Defence Department's Advanced Research Project Agency to build *Battlezone*, a training simulator for tank drivers. It is unclear if they ever actually used *Battlezone,* but certainly this set a precedent.

During the same decade the army built SIMNET (SIMulator NETworking) to encourage collaborative training and to replace live exercises and costly equipment (van der Graaf and Nieborg 2003). In 1996 the American Marines modified *Doom* (1993) to produce *Marine Doom*, a version which removed all unrealistic weapons and introduced four-man fire teams, reflecting a formation that the army uses in reality. *Flight Simulator* (1989) was also used as a training tool by both the American army and purportedly the terrorist pilots of the September 11 airplanes. Arguably the relationship between the digital games industry and the military has deepened in the last decade. The use by the American military of digital games and simulators has moved beyond commissioning games companies to develop training simulations and versions of commercial games to the establishment of in-house gaming expertise and the development of original games to use as promotion and recruitment devices.

The American military funded and co-developed *America's Army* (2002), an online multiplayer PC game which departs from conventional strategies in the PC segment of the industry in that it is only available online and player modifications are not encouraged. The game is however free to download and indications are that it has contributed significantly to recruitment levels and brand awareness (van der Graaf and Nieborg 2003). Developed by a team of professional developers, researchers and students at the Naval Postgraduate School (California) and using the UnReal engine, it cost $7.2 million to develop. No doubt its marketing budget was also significant as the army brought real personnel carriers and a helicopter to E3 in 2004 to promote the game, one of the main international trade shows for the games and entertainment industry (See www.americasarmy.com/).

Another example of the deepening relationship between the military and the entertainment industry, including digital games is provided by the Institute for Creative Technologies (ICT), at the University of Southern California. The Pentagon invested $44 million in ICT to bring together a group of Hollywood executives, game designers and businessmen to establish a think-tank on future combat systems and immersive training simulations. The investment resulted in *Full Spectrum Warrior* (2003), a game which is used both for training by the army and is available commercially.[1] While the military has always used the media to advertise and recruit, packaging the military training experience into a sanitised entertainment experience is a rather ironic complement to the power of modern computing to depict 'realistic

IMAGE 14 *America's Army: Operations* (2002), image provided courtesy of the US Army.

situations'. It also brings to the fore the degree to which ideology is embedded in digital games.

DIGITAL GAMES AND LEARNING IN INFORMAL CONTEXTS

We have seen that introducing digital games into formal educational contexts, particularly at primary and secondary levels, is more an aspiration than a reality at present. However, at the same time, third-level institutions and the private sector are using digital games and simulations for a variety of purposes. Of course, not all education and learning takes place in formal contexts and game players invest a lot of their leisure time into learning to play games like *Civilization III* (2001) and *America's Army: Operations* (2002) in non-work contexts.

Gee (2003) argues that in good games, players consciously engage in critical learning and that this form of learning is transferable to other contexts. If this is the case, then digital game play in informal contexts is valuable in terms of people's existence in everyday life. Certainly those who sell home PCs would have us believe that buying a home PC is an important investment in education. Indeed, governments who promote concepts like the 'information superhighway' or the 'information society' often use language and arguments of a similar nature. However, a counter argument is that the site of learning has an important influence on the type of learning which takes place and that not everyone will be able to engage in critical learning due to factors which are external to the digital games.

There is very little evidence as yet to support the claim that the critical learning skills which may be used in certain games are transferable to other contexts. Certainly there are studies that show that digital games encourage critical learning, but they stop short of claiming that this learning is transferable. Kerr et al. (2004) found instances of critical learning through digital game play in a pilot study of adult and children players in the home. In this study players tended to discard manuals and engage in trial-and-error, practice and repetition. Other studies point to the value of both spectating and discussing tactics with others in relation to learning to play (Sefton-Green and Buckingham 1998; McFarlane et al. 2002; Newman 2002b; Ermi and Mäyrä 2003). However, none of these studies investigated the transferability of these learning skills to other contexts.

What does emerge from current studies is the fact that the site of learning, even in informal contexts, can influence the types of learning that take place. PC game play in particular is influenced by the attention/ resources devoted to software, technical support, position of the technology in the home, and family/household relationships. As we saw in the last chapter, research has found that game play and game talk in non-formal contexts is more embedded in boy's leisure culture than that of girls and it is argued that this may influence access and use patterns (Vered 1998; McFarlane et al. 2002). What is made clear in these studies is that contextual and gender issues cannot be ignored when considering the education and learning potential of digital games in non-formal contexts.

Studies of teenagers, education and learning have also found that there may be a limit to the potential of self-directed learning using PCs. A UK project conducted with teenagers in their homes found that children rarely engaged in creative or technically complex activities like programming with home computers (Sefton-Green and Buckingham 1998). This study found that while many teenagers learnt to use software programs 'by doing', a teacher-type figure, a parent, relative or peer, was important in terms of progressing this use to a more creative and complex level. Further, this study found that the creative use of computing was more likely to be done by male teenagers. The study concluded that:

> without the social envelope surrounding the use of home computers, genuine 'educational computing' will be as rare as the creative users of computers we set out to discover – for reasons which are to do with limitations of software, with economics and with parental guidance and control. (Sefton-Green and Buckingham 1998: 82)

Interviews with parents provide conflicting evidence, although some of these studies are very small scale and it is hard to construct a general picture. McFarlane et al. (2002: 21) found that parents felt that games contributed to developing skills such as problem solving, design, strategy, co-operation and hand–eye co-ordination. Further, they viewed the fact that digital games encouraged social discourse as a strong positive factor. By contrast, Livingstone (2002b; 2003: 153) found that adults were not persuaded as to the pedagogic value of their children playing digital games and were uncertain and in some cases anxious about the relationship between education and entertainment.

GOVERNMENT PROMOTION OF MEDIA LITERACY AND DIGITAL GAME PLAY

Livingstone (2002b: 215) argues elsewhere that the growing commercialisation and privatisation of domestic leisure has meant that the boundary between education and entertainment and between leisure and work/school is increasingly blurred. As a result there is much more pressure to evaluate leisure-time activities in terms of their contribution to work and education. This trend may be hastened by government policies in some countries to transfer more of the responsibility for policing ICT use onto what are now called 'citizen-consumers'. The move to promote 'media literacy' has emerged at the nexus of debates about the need to address the digital divide and to promote lifelong learning but is equally about the rolling back of state regulation in favour of audience/user education and freedom of choice. Within this debate the role of educators and schools is being rethought, as is the concept of literacy itself.

Literacy used to be associated with reading, writing and arithmetic, but the development of new media calls for a redefinition and broadening of the concept, and the need to think instead about multiple literacies. For Kellner, literacy means 'gaining competencies in effectively using socially constructed forms of communication and representation' and involves 'gaining the skills and knowledge to read and interpret the text of the world' (Kellner 2002: 91). He sees literacy as a necessary precondition for navigating and negotiating life. Livingstone has a slightly broader interpretation of media literacy which involves 'the ability to access, analyse, evaluate and create messages across a variety of contexts' (2002a: 1).

This broader definition, which includes the ability to 'create' or 'produce' one's own messages as well as the ability to access, critically analyse and evaluate the work of others, is the basis for the following definition used by OFCOM, the telecommunications and broadcasting regulator in the UK: 'media literacy is the ability to access, understand and create communications in a variety of contexts' (OFCOM 2004). Already the productive element of this definition is being explored, whereby students in formal learning contexts are being taught how to develop their own games. A number of projects in the UK are currently developing prototype game-authoring software aimed at allowing children to produce their own role-playing and adventure games (Edge

2004c; Hayes 2004). OFCOM hope to work with a variety of stake-holders to collate an evidence base of research barriers to media literacy, to assess current levels of media literacy in the UK, and to ensure that labelling on media products is clear and accurate. Future policies on media literacy in the UK will undoubtedly influence how digital games are integrated into formal contexts.

Despite the paucity of empirical evidence in educational and media studies to show that learning in digital games in formal and informal contexts is transferable to other contexts, it is clear that digital games are deemed useful as learning tools in a number of contexts. This is not to ignore the fact that some psychological studies argue that digital games do teach people skills and knowledge that are transferable into the everyday world and that people learn from, as well as with, digital games. Such findings are often taken out of context and used to provide emotive moral and political capital which follows particular instances of violent social behaviour. The use of academic studies in this way can be examined in detail in the online transcriptions of the hearings before the American Senate following the Columbine High School shootings (Jenkins 1999).

Psychological studies of the potential effects of playing violent digital games draw upon a number of theories ranging from catharsis (i.e. the theory that playing violent video games may help to release aggressive behaviour impulses) to learning and social learning theories. It is the latter which is particularly relevant here as social learning theory asserts people learn to behave by modelling what they directly observe and experience (Bandura 1977). The argument in relation to digital games is that digital game players, particularly children, may learn to behave and act in ways that they have directly observed and experienced in digital games. Psychological studies of violent video games and children suggest that a small percentage of game players have 'special vulnerability' and therefore exposure to realistic violence may trigger aggressive behaviour (Griffiths 1991, 1997; Funk 2002). It is also suggested that immersion or absorption in digital games may lead to a suspension of rational thought and the development of 'aggressive behavioural scripts'. One survey of research in the area concluded that: 'There is developing support for the contention that playing violent electronic games is associated with less pro-social behaviour in children, including increased aggression and lower empathy' (Funk 2002: 134).

Current psychological studies, however, provide a very problematic, contradictory and fragmented evidence base from which to draw any conclusions. It appears that for the majority of game players, playing violent digital games has no significant effect (Buckingham 2002; Bryce and Rutter 2003). This is not to say that they have no effect, but rather that current studies are unable to map exactly the nature and direction of that effect. Further, the reliance on surveys, self-reporting or laboratory experiments have tended to downplay the mediating influence of context and sociality, to focus on short-term effects, to ignore player skills/competence, and to use a wide range of definitions of violence. Moreover, there is little exploration of the role of culture and the fact that certain types of violent computer games do not sell well in certain markets, for example, Japan.

This critique of current psychological studies of violence and digital games should come as no surprise, given the emphasis on the diversity of digital games and the social and cultural differences between contexts of play and players which we have encountered in previous chapters. In addition, game studies has only begun to delineate and map the experience of game playing and map the pleasures and displeasures involved in the relationship between game, game system, player and context. It is not surprising therefore that many psychological studies show conflicting results, whereby even the definition of particular genres and of degrees and types of 'violence' are contested. However, it is also not an outright dismissal of such work. As elsewhere, there is a need to adapt established research methods to take into account the specificities of digital games as text, industry and culture. The emerging generation of digital games researchers and students have an insider's knowledge of digital games and will be in a stronger position than researchers heretofore to critique the content and experience of digital games as well as to understand the rapidly developing and changing contours of their place in society.

SUMMARY

It is apparent that digital games have moved beyond entertainment and even edutainment to become tools for learning in different contexts. While the theories and evidence base are disputed, it is recognised that digital games are useful in certain situations for certain purposes.

However, it is far from clear how best to deploy them, what type of critical learning is taking place, and how transferable that is from virtual to real spaces. What is certain is that researchers in different fields need to adapt their research methods and work together in order to understand the digital game/user/context relationship.

NOTE

1 Thanks to Ed Halter, film critic for the *Village Voice* and Founder/Director of the New York Underground Film Festival, who gave a presentation entitled 'War Games: Digital Gaming and the US Military' in Dublin, Ireland on 25 May 2004. See www.imagesfestival.com/2004/programs/war_games.asp.

SEVEN
CONCLUSION

This book set out to explore digital games as texts and the processes involved in their production and consumption in order to assess the implications for media and social theories. It also set out to establish just how 'global' and 'new' digital games really are. One of the starting points for this book was the belief that if the media are 'systems for the production, distribution and consumption of symbolic forms' (Garnham 2000: 39), then the digital games industry can be situated within the wider media system and regarded as an emergent and dynamic set of institutions, forms and practices. We have established so far that the digital games industry is indeed a growing economic activity involving a range of institutions in different countries producing a variety of symbolic forms. Further, we have established that digital games provide new social spaces and stimulate new social practices but that these are shaped by wider social and cultural structures and may indeed serve to reinforce existing stereotype ideologies and inequalities. Thus any discussion of digital games must start by appreciating their diversity, flexibility, the degree of agency and control afforded to the user and the variations in use between different social and cultural contexts. In what follows I shall briefly reflect on the implications of the findings for media and social theory more generally.

IMPLICATIONS FOR MEDIA THEORY

OUR UNDERSTANDING OF THE MEDIA TEXT

Digital games must be situated within the wider context of new media, a loosely defined grouping of new techno-cultural forms united by their digital nature, convergence, new forms of engagement and networked characteristics. Of course, even old media are now becoming new as, for example, traditional analogue television becomes digitised, and the relationship between old and new is ever more complex and synergetic.

Nevertheless, as media texts, digital games lay down some important challenges to established media theories. The ludology/narratology debate referred to in Chapter 2 may have lost some of its vigour but it points to the problems faced by academics who operate within particular disciplinary frameworks and whose careers depend on engaging with, and operating within, existing institutional settings. Indeed, it emerges in our analysis that narratology is internally diverse and undergoing extension and revision in the light of changing media forms. However, there is an emerging consensus amongst game theorists that rules, goals, space, time, modes of engagement and control operate in fundamentally different ways in digital games than in other media and are potentially more important to an understanding of digital games than narrative.

Similarly, there is an ongoing debate as to the application of representation theories in this new domain and to the differences between characters in a film or television programme and playable avatars in a digital game. This is not to say that representations are not important, and certainly as it was argued in Chapter 2, the circulation of images in meta-texts surrounding a game, including the packaging and marketing materials, plays an important role in situating the game for the fan and non-fan alike. However, for the game player, the avatars' capabilities coupled to their representation are formative and there appear to be interesting differences between MMOGs and other games in this regard and even between situations within an MMOG. For example, while one's capabilities may play an important role in terms of one's usefulness within a team on a particular mission, one's representation may also play an important role in terms of one's attractiveness to other players in non-combat situations. The latter appears to be an important motivation particularly in Asian online role-playing games.

An important issue for media scholars is the variability and flexibility of the digital game as media text. This has implications not only for understanding them as a media form but also for studying players' pleasures and their interactions with particular texts. The argument that we need to move beyond our two-level model of media texts to a three-level model illustrates the impact digital games and interactive texts more generally are having on media theory. It is clear that the close coupling of the text/medium/player in the game play experience and the potential variability of the text signal a need to combine different research methods in order to understand the different meanings and experiences afforded by a text to different players.

OUR UNDERSTANDING OF MEDIA PRODUCTION AND THE CULTURAL INDUSTRIES

The digital game industry is clearly global in its reach: its networks of production exploit geography, time and deregulated working regimes to produce products and services for particular markets. As in other cultural industries, there are clear examples of how the industry has employed post-Fordist structures and processes of flexible accumulation. But this is far from universal and there is conflicting evidence as to the 'flexibility' of development companies, particularly third-party companies, who generally employ a core salaried staff. Indeed, this inflexibility is sometimes given as a reason for the high rate of company failures and reformations as companies run into cashflow problems between projects.

Further, there is also a strong trend, as identified in Chapter 3, towards vertical integration and the development of first-party or in-house production teams in publishers. What evidence exists would suggest that the cultures of production in many development firms are both flexible and highly pressurised with intense periods of work at crunch or deadline time. Other evidence would suggest it is a largely male-dominated and masculine culture. Thus the picture that emerges is one of contradictions and diversity, in line with Harvey's (1989: 196) observation about new forms of 'temporal and spatial' fixes to ongoing capitalist crises.

What is more evident is that digital games can be situated within the wider cultural industries and display many of the key characteristics and strategies seen in other cultural industries. In Chapter 3 we dealt with three characteristics in particular: the high levels of risk involved in a hit-driven business; the high production and low reproduction costs involved in cultural production; and the similarity of cultural products to public goods. These characteristics motivate cultural industries in general, and the digital games industry in particular, to maximise economies of scale and scope and motivate the development of business strategies aimed at controlling and managing creative labour, guaranteeing the continuous supply of content, and maximising returns on that content across various media platforms. As in other media businesses, there is a conflict between cultivating player productivity (e.g. through modding, blogging, fansites) and policing consumer behaviour (e.g. through regional variations in disks, lock-out chips, end user licence agreements (EULAs) and active pursuit of 'pirates').

A key argument expounded in Chapter 3 is that we need to consider and understand the relationship between, and the internal dynamics of, different subsectors within the digital games industry. While console games constitute the largest segment of the industry in terms of sales in the USA and Japan, this is not the case in other countries. Furthermore, while not as significant yet in terms of sales, both MMOGs and mini games on a variety of platforms are clearly emergent and growing subsectors. We examined the differences in terms of market concentration, revenue models, underlying technological platform and production processes between console games, standard PC games, MMOGs and mini games. This typology takes us away from existing hardware-based typologies and will allow for the emergence of new hybrid technologies and the addition of new segments. What emerges from this analysis is that while the organisation of production in the console and PC segments are comparable to the book publishing and film production processes, the production of MMOGs is a more complex process, tending more towards the broadcasting model. By comparison, success in the mini games subsector seems to be based on the rapid turnaround of multiple products, although these products are less perishable than a press product.

It emerged from an analysis of recent trends in the digital games industry that various forms of consolidation are taking place, including examples of vertical, horizontal and diagonal integration. Furthermore, it is becoming increasingly difficult for third-party developers to publish a game on the main console platforms, a trend likely to be exacerbated by the next-generation of consoles to be launched in 2005/06. Not only have the main publishers bought many of their competitors and bought into development companies, but they are also looking to produce cross-platform titles, sequels, movie and TV-tie-ins and merchandising to maximise profits. For third-party companies, there are various means available – including working for hire for publishers, conducting outsourcing work for super-developers, developing PC/mini games, and pursuing alternative sources of funding – by which they are trying to survive. At least this appears to be the situation in the USA and the UK; there is less written about the situation in Asia.

Chapter 4 provided some more detail on the challenges faced by development companies at various stages of the production cycle, including the search for capital, the search for staff, the negotiation of a contract with a publisher and the struggle to maintain creative control over the project. It is clear that there is an ongoing struggle between publishers and developers for creative control, although this depends on the reputation and track record of the developer. The well-known development studios, such as Blizzard or id Software, have much better bargaining power than an unknown company. This struggle for power is key to understanding the production of a digital game across all segments but particularly in the console segment.

A related issue which is of interest to media scholars is that of authorship. While individual 'auteurs', or game designers or programmers, achieve fame and a degree of symbolic power, it is clear from our analysis of the production process and the division of labour in an typical development company that game development is a collaborative process involving complex negotiations between a team of people (sometimes up to 100) and their publisher.

Raymond Williams, in *The Sociology of Culture* (1981), identifies four different institutional forms of cultural production which specify different relations between the cultural producer and the market: artisanal, post-artisanal, market professional and corporate professional. Digital game companies have moved rapidly from the artisanal stage evident in its early days to the market professional stage and to an even larger extent the corporate professional stage. It is clear that the direct commissioning of work by publishers and the development of game concepts in-house by the publisher are becoming ever more prevalent, particularly in the console segment. Meanwhile, one still finds some degree of post-artisanal forms in the mini-games segment, where individuals and small companies sell their games to intermediate aggregators. Finally, pockets of artisanal development are to be found in the independent or 'indie' game development sector, which produces games and then tries to secure a publishing deal or sell direct to the consumer.

FROM AUDIENCES TO PLAYERS

The analysis in Chapter 5 of who plays digital games, what pleasures they gain from the experience, and where they play them, allows us to extrapolate how digital game play might offer new experiences and indeed influence existing media practices. What is clear from the large surveys discussed in Chapter 5 is that, while levels of access to consoles and PC are relatively high in the USA, the UK, Japan and a number of other countries, playing patterns are diverse. Furthermore, only a small number of total players could be termed heavy or enthusiastic players and the amount of time they spend playing games, according to some of the surveys, does not even approach average television consumption. As with established media, digital game play is marked by certain age, sex and class differences in the USA and the UK. However, when digital game play is contextualised in terms of overall media use, it appears that in certain instances it is having a significant influence on patterns of domestic television and computer use as well as household negotiations over access to these media.

Empirical research studies suggest that networked play and MMOGs are leading to the development of entirely new spaces and patterns of interactive media practice. For example, LAN parties at internet cafes and at other venues are an important feature of digital game play and involve a high degree of social interaction both on- and offline. MMOG studies have found that people often spend as much, if not more, time socialising as on quests. The pleasures of playing digital games certainly appear to differ to some degree from the pleasures offered by traditional media, but they also vary between subsectors as well as between contexts and cultures. It appears that control, exploration, performance, sociability/community and, to a lesser extent, narrative are important component aspects of digital game play, although their importance varies from player to player and game to game. Far from being a totally interactive experience, digital game play involves a range of modes of engagement from hands-on play, to menu browsing, to watching others play. It also invites varying degrees of transformative play or player creativity, ranging from cheating to modding and hacking, which seems to shift play from habitual to reflexive engagement.

This survey of digital game player research highlights the overall simplicity of industry discussions which focus on just two archetypal players: hardcore and casual. Digital game play research indicates that people play in different ways at different times of their lives and depending on their changing levels of competency. Digital game play is also influenced by a number of contextual factors, including cultural constructions, physical location of the technology, domestic structure, social networks, perceptions and the wider discourse about digital games. It would be unwise to overstate the significance of access rates as compared to studies of actual use. It is knowledge of the latter which the industry and academics should be actively pursuing. One might think that dormant, disinterested and prospective game players should be at least as attractive in research terms as what are called 'hardcore players' for both the industry and academics.

It is interesting to see the gradual emergence of a debate about the usefulness of digital games as learning and educational tools in a variety of contexts, while also observing the vilification of digital games in other fora. In France certain types of digital games receive government funding from the National Film Board, in Korea the government promotes digital game play as part of the wider media culture, and in the UK digital games are included in the media studies syllabi at secondary level. However, in other countries the debate is more about censorship, regulation and the negative effects of digital game play.

A short course in media history will establish that these struggles between different interest groups to frame what is 'new' in either wholly negative or wholly positive terms has a long pedigree. Nevertheless, the argument for strong media effects which emerged alongside the emergence of the mass media has been undermined by years of media research and indeed games research. Such research highlights the diversity of experiences which different players can have with particular games and the intervening influence of personal, contextual and historical factors. The same issues confront those seeking to evaluate the learning potential of digital games and the extent to which skills and knowledge are transferable from virtual to real situations. What is clear is that digital games are being used in certain contexts particularly for motivational and communicative purposes and that as research starts to illuminate the user/text/context relationship we will come to understand better the usefulness and limitations of digital games as learning tools.

IMPLICATIONS FOR SOCIAL THEORY

GLOBAL PRODUCTION AND LOCAL CONSUMPTION

This book attempts to situate the emerging digital games industry within the context of the increasingly liberalised and commercialised media, the increasingly global production networks of multinational corporations and the unequal access to, and use of, new information and communication technologies between and within different societies. While it is clear that the networks that produce digital games are transnational and that they are largely self-regulated in their main markets, it is also clear that games produced for one culture may not sell well in another. This points to the complex relationship between global flows and local cultural practices, which is a key challenge to transnational cultural organisations and undermines any simplistic conceptualisation of cultural imperialism.

For example, some research indicates that many Asians find game environments designed in the USA and UK too dark and perceive the characters as ugly, while for many in the USA and the UK certain Japanese game genres like romance games seem foreign. While the majority of games are produced in English and Japanese, it is evident that games produced in other countries may not make it onto the main console platforms if it is not considered financially feasible to localise them. While major effort goes into the localisation of digital games to enable simultaneous shipping to occur in different markets, and so reduce piracy rates, simultaneous shipping may mean that translation has to be done without the visual context needed for good quality work; indeed, finding a translator who understands games and their conventions is a very real barrier (O'Hagan and Mangiron 2004). In addition, games need to be adapted to local cultural and legal specificities. This includes changing the colour of blood in Germany to green and altering the Japanese version of *Tomb Raider* so that avatars run out of time rather than die. Finally, MMOGs and networked games also introduce a range of cross-cultural communication issues which need to be addressed and players will usually choose more local servers to play on as a result.

It is interesting to consider the intersection of these technological, organisational, financial and cultural issues in relation to the political economy theories introduced at the beginning of this book. The pressures exerted by the need for simultaneous translation and the difficulties introduced by the linguistic and cultural differences between different markets result in very real obstacles to the circulation of particular games outside their home markets. Indeed, only a small number of digital games sell outside their home markets. This signals that it is not only the ownership and increasing concentration of publishers and the need to control creative personnel that is causing the lack of original games but cultural barriers as well. Coupled with the very real barriers to entry encountered by developers outside the core development markets, one can begin to understand the complex range of determinants influencing the trend towards sequels, licensing and in-house productions. It is not simply a matter of economics, or at least not solely.

What implications do these observations have in terms of our understanding of the role of the media within wider globalisation processes? First, I would argue that while technologically it is possible to play with gamers from anywhere in the world and to play products from a range of different cultures, a range of business and cultural factors act to impede the circulation of these products in a truly 'global' sense. Thus, while the media may enable global flows, this is not sufficient to create global media spaces and products. Second, while the economic production of cultural products may depend upon transnational networks, there are clear persistent inequalities in terms of who can access and play these games and where. Digital game playing is not a transnational activity in any sense, the main markets are currently the USA, certain countries in Europe, Japan and South Korea. Third, despite the possibilities offered by ICTs in terms of mobility and teleworking, the centres of the digital game industry remain in LA, London and Tokyo, which underscores the importance of these centres in terms of global distribution and global financial flows. Fourth, while digital games invite transformative play, empowerment and identity play, the digital games industry works hard to ensure that these transformations are not exploited in any way by game players for profit (see Postigo 2003). Moreover, unless one has particular technological skills, the identities that one is offered may be extremely culturally specific and limited.

In sum, the digital games industry mirrors other media industries in terms of being controlled by a small number of transnational corporations operating from a small number of centres. Their products are developed for a small number of large markets and localised for other markets. It is only in the smaller and highly competitive PC and mini-games segments that one finds a greater diversity of content as well as a diversity of producers. It is also here that one finds examples of companies, artists and players engaging in transformative, political and reflexive play and production. Unfortunately, it is particularly difficult for companies to survive in these subsectors. In the MMOG subsegment one also finds interesting examples of community player power challenging corporations to revise, reform and update game services. This points to the emergence of something that is not merely a play space but perhaps to some degree a political space, where players can exert some influence over how the space is run.

GENDER AND TECHNOLOGY

A major problem faced by the digital games industry relates to gender in general and the inclusion of women more specifically – an issue that is highlighted throughout the book. Given the origins of the digital games industry in public science research labs and electronics firms, perhaps it is unsurprising that it was initially dominated by male programmer/scientists and that most of the early games were based on themes of war and conquest. What is less defensible is that the industry, particularly in the USA and the UK, continues to be dominated by male employees, that its trade fairs and advertising should trade so explicitly in heterosexual male fantasies and that many public game-playing spaces are seen as 'chilly' places to hang out by many females and some males. We cannot separate the gender structure in the industry from gender symbolism in and surrounding games and the individual gender of game players and game designers (Kerr 2002).

Many academics argue that gender is a fluid social construct which is constructed by and through practice (Aune 1996; Cassell and Jenkins 1998; Lie 1998; Oudshoorn et al. 2004). Particular technologies do not have an 'essential' gender, rather it emerges from a process of negotiation and stabilises into a common interpretation. Thus there is no essential reason why women should not be fully represented in the computer and IT industries and in the consumption cultures based upon them. There is no essential reason why the digital games industry should be seen as masculine, that digital games should tend towards a particular form of masculinity or that digital game playing should be seen as an unnatural female pastime. There is also no reason why it cannot be changed. Yet for many outside the industry and gaming culture it is seen as an exclusively male pastime, and for many within the industry and culture this is the 'natural' state of affairs, despite the industry's claims of the opposite.

This topic is highly emotive both for researchers and the industry and the theme is returned to again and again throughout the book. It emerges when one examines the origins of the digital games industry and when one looks at data on the overall representation of women in the industry. It emerges as a topic when one examines the production cycle and the working culture in development companies. It emerges in studies of the representation of masculinity and femininity in digital games and in discussions about the language and images used to market those games. It emerges in discussions with publishers and developers who want to reach the 'mass market' but are rather unclear how to do this. Finally, it emerges in studies of digital game play in different contexts. While some girls and women enjoy playing digital games and adopt particular strategies to deal with, and appropriate, the given representations if they offend them, others merely engage with abstract games like puzzles or exclude this particular cultural activity from their leisure time altogether. Increasingly, researchers are starting to discover that asking people if they are 'gamers' may not be the best approach given the social meanings that are currently attached to this term.

Indeed, it is impossible to write about digital games and to ignore gender. It will soon be a decade since Cassell and Jenkins first wrote about gender and computer games (1998) and we have seen the coming and going of Purple Moon, the arrival of a pink Game Boy Advance (GBA) and the establishment by the International Game Development Association (IGDA) of a 'Women in Game Development' committee. Yet the evidence suggests that we have a lot of work to do in order to understand the ways in which the digital games field continues to gender itself with a particular form of masculinity while at the same time adopting a discourse of gender neutrality and even some attempts to design games for women.

My initial studies indicate that relying on expert game players as testers, general market surveys, registered users and designers who are avid game players is tending to replicate the overall structure of the industry. Attempts to design games specifically for women, however, tend to veer towards stereotypes and essentialist qualities and may alienate as many women as they attract. Anecdotal evidence would suggest that this gendering process does not appear to operate in the same way in countries like Japan and South Korea. More research is required to explain why this is the case. This task becomes even more urgent given the desire by certain bodies to introduce digital games into non-entertainment sectors like education, training, recruitment and health.

Digital games as work and as play are becoming increasingly prevalent in certain cultures. As scholars of the media, we need to recognise and take seriously the important role that digital games play in the lives of our students and our colleagues. We need to recognise the subtle and not so subtle influence they are having on the design, diffusion and use of other media. We also need to begin to question and interrogate the influence they are having on wider patterns of communication, on the construction and reconstruction of cultures and on social relationships. This book has been an attempt to open the black box and allow people to peer inside at some of the complexities of digital games as texts, as industry and as cultural practice. Much more work remains to be done.

REFERENCES

Aarseth, E. (1997) *Cybertext. Perspectives on Ergodic Literature*. Baltimore and London, Johns Hopkins University Press.

Aarseth, E. (2001) 'Computer game studies, year one.' *Game Studies* 1(1).

Aarseth, E. (2004) 'Genre trouble: narrativism and the art of simulation', in N. Wardrip-Fruin and P. Harrigan (eds), *First Person. New Media as Story, Performance and Game*. Cambridge, MA, MIT Press: 45–55.

Adorno, T. and M. Gurevitch (1977) 'The culture industry: enlightenment as mass deception', in J. Curran (ed.), *Mass Communication and Society*. London, Edward Arnold in association with the Open University Press.

Adorno, T. and M. Horkheimer (1979) *Dialectic of Enlightenment*. London, Verso.

Akrich, M. (1992) 'The De-scription of technical objects', in W. Bijker and J. Law (eds), *Shaping Technology/Building Society. Studies in Socio-Technical Change*. Cambridge, MA, MIT Press: 205–24.

Akrich, M. (1995) 'User representations: practices, methods and sociology', in A. Rip, T. Misa and S. Johan (eds), *Managing Technology in Society*. London, Pinter: 167–84.

Akrich, M. and B. Latour (1992) 'A summary of a convenient vocabulary for the semiotics of human and non-human assemblies', in W. Bijker and J. Law (eds), *Shaping Technology/Building Society: Studies in Sociotechnical Change*. Cambridge, MA, MIT Press: 259–64.

Alloway, N. and P. Gilbert (1998) 'Video game culture: playing with masculinity, violence and pleasure', in S. Howard (ed.), *Wired-Up: Young People and Electronic Media*. London, UCL Press: 95–114.

Alvisi, A., A. Narduzzo, and M. Zamerian (2003) 'Squint-eyed strategies for success: Playstation and the power of unexpected consequences', *Information, Communication and Society* 6(4): 608–27.

Amin, A. (ed.) (1994) *Post-Fordism. A Reader*. Studies in Urban and Social Change. Oxford and Cambridge, MA, Blackwell.

Ang, I. (1996) *Living Room Wars. Rethinking Media Audiences for a Postmodern World*. London and New York, Routledge.

Aoyama, Y. and H. Izushi (2003) 'Hardware gimmick or cultural innovation? Technological, cultural and social foundations of the Japanese video game industry'. *Research Policy* 32: 423–44.

Asakura, R. (2000) *Revolutionaries at Sony: The Making of the Sony Playstation and the Visionaries Who Conquered the World of Video Games*. New York, McGraw-Hill.

Atkins, B. (2003) *More than a Game: The Computer Game as Fictional Form*. Manchester, Manchester University Press.

Aune, M. (1996) 'The computer in everyday life: patterns of domestication of a new technology', in M. Lie and K. Sørensen (eds), *Making Technology Our Own? Domesticating Technology into Everyday Life*. Oslo and Oxford, Scandinavian University Press.

Avedon, E. M. and B. Sutton-Smith (eds) (1971) *The Study of Games*. New York, John Wiley & Sons.

Bandura, A. (1977) *Social Learning Theory*. Englewood Cliffs, NJ, Prentice-Hall.

Barthes, R. (1970) *S/Z*. Paris, Editions du Seuil.

Barthes, R. (1977) *Image, Music, Text*. London, Fontana.

Behrendt, W., G. Geser, A. Mulrenin and S. Reich (2003) 'EP2010 – The future of electronic publishing towards 2010.' Retrieved 12/12/03, 2003, from ep2010.salzburgresearch.at

Bolter, D. J. and R. Grusin (2000) *Remediation. Understanding New Media*. Cambridge, MA, MIT Press.

Bourdieu, P. (1994) *Distinction*. London, Routledge.

Bryce, J. and J. Rutter (2002a) 'Killing like a girl: gendered gaming and girl gamers' visibility', in F. Mayra (ed.), *Computer Games and Digital Cultures*. Tampere, Tampere University Press.

Bryce, J. and J. Rutter (2002b) 'Spectacle of the deathmatch: character and narrative in first-person shooters', in G. King and T. Krzywinska (eds), *ScreenPlay. Cinema/Videogames/Interfaces*. London, Wallflower Press: 66–80.

Bryce, J. and J. Rutter (2003) 'Gender dynamics and the social and spatial organisation of computer gaming', *Leisure Studies* 22: 1–15.

Buckingham, D. (2002) 'The electronic generation? Children and new media', in L. A. Lievrouw, and S. Livingstone (eds), *Handbook of New Media*. London, Sage: 77–89.

Buckingham, D. and J. Sefton-Green (2003) 'Gotta catch'em all. Structure, agency and pedagogy in children's media culture'. *Media, Culture and Society* 25: 379–99.

Caillois, R. (2001) *Man, Play and Games*. Urbana, University of Illinois Press.

Carr, D. (2002) 'Playing with Lara' in G. King and T. Krzywinska (eds), *ScreenPlay. Cinema/Videogames/Interfaces*. London, Wallflower Press: 171–11.

Carr, D., Burn, A., Schot, G. and Buckingham, D. (2003) 'Textuality in Video Games' in M. Copier and J. Raessens (eds), *Level Up: Digital Games Research Conference Proceedings*. Utrecht, University of Utrecht Press.

Cassell, J. and H. Jenkins, (eds) (1998) *From Barbie to Mortal Kombat: Gender and Computer Games*. Cambridge, MA, MIT Press.

Castells, M. (2000) *The Rise of the Network Society*. Oxford, Blackwell.

CESA (2002) *Games White Paper*. Tokyo, Computer Entertainment Software Association.

Chatman, Seymour (1978) *Story and Discourse: Narrative Structure in Fiction and Film*. Ithaca, NY, and London, Cornell University Press.

Consalvo, M. (2003a) 'Cyber-slaying media fans: code, digital poaching and corporate control of the internet'. *Journal of Communication Inquiry* 27(1): 67–86.

Consalvo, M. (2003b) 'Hot dates and fairy-tale romances. Studying sexuality in video games'. In M. Wolf and B. Perron (eds), *The Video Game Theory Reader*. London, Routledge: 171–220.

Cook, P. (ed.) (1985) *The Cinema Book*. London, BFI.

Coombs, R., K. Green, A. Richards and V. Walsh (eds) (2001) *Technology and the Market. Demand, Users and Innovation.* Cheltenham, UK, and Northampton, MA, Edward Elgar.

Cornford, J., R. Naylor and S. Driver (2000) 'New media and regional development: the case of the UK computer and video games industry', in A. Giunta, A. Lagendijk and A. Pike (eds), *Restructuring Industry and Territory. The Experience of Europe's Regions.* London, Stationery Office: 83–108.

Cubitt, S. (1998) *Digital Aesthetics.* London, Sage.

Cubitt, S. (2001) *Simulation and Social Theory.* London, Sage.

Darley, A. (2000) *Visual Digital Culture. Surface Play and Spectacle in New Media Genres.* London, Routledge.

DataMonitor (2002) *Global Electronic Games, 2001–2007. Riding the Next Generation Wave.* London, DataMonitor Corporation.

Davenport, H. (2002) 'Is learning just a game? The teachers view.' Retrieved 20/11/04, from www.nestafuturelab.org/articles/learn02.htm

DEG (2005) 'Industry boosted by $21.2 billion in annual DVD sales and rentals'. Los Angeles, Digital Entertainment Group, *DVD News*, 6 January.

Deutsche Bank (2002) *The Video Games Industry. Game Over or Extended Play?* Frankfurt, Deutsche Bank.

DFC Intelligence (2004) *The Business of Computer and Video Games.* March.

Dodson, S. (2004) 'Let the games begin'. *Guardian*, 16 November.

Doyle, G. (2002) *Understanding Media Economics.* London, Sage.

DTI (2001) *The UK Games Industry and Higher Education Final Report.* London, Department of Trade and Industry.

Du Gay, P., S. Hall L. Janes, H. Mackay and K. Negus (eds) (1997) *Doing Cultural Studies: The Story of the Sony Walkman.* Culture, Media and Identities Series. London, Sage, in association with the Open University.

Edge (2003a) 'The future of independents'. *Edge.* September: 7–9.

Edge (2003b) 'The state of play nation'. *Edge.* February: 7–9.

Edge (2004a) 'Advergaming: a lifeline for developers?' *Edge*: 10–11.

Edge (2004b) 'Different strokes'. *Edge.* February: 60–6.

Edge (2004c) 'Institute honours gaming benefits'. *Edge*: 13.

Edge (2004d) 'Land Ahoy. Lara Croft creator Toby Gard's ship is finally coming in: Confounding Factor's Galleon will be released by SCI in May'. *Edge.* February: 55–9.

Edquist, C. (ed.) (1997) *Systems of Innovations: Technologies, Institutions and Organisations.* London, Pinter.

Egenfeldt-Nielsen, S. (2004) 'Practical barriers in using educational computer games'. *On the Horizon* 12(1): 18–21.

Ermi, L. and F. Mäyrä (2003) 'Power and control of games: children as the actors of game cultures'. In M. Copier and J. Raessens (eds), *Level Up: Digital Games Research Conference Proceedings.* Utrecht, University of Utrecht Press.

ESA (2003) *Industry Sales and Economic Data, 2003.* Consumer Spending Poll, Entertainment Software Association.

ESA (2004) *Essential Facts about the Computer and Video Game Industry.* Washington, Entertainment Software Association.

Eskelinen, M. (2004) 'Towards computer game studies', in N. Wardrip-Fruin and P. Harrigan (eds), *First Person. New Media as Story, Performance and Game.* Cambridge, MA, MIT Press: 36–44.

Filiciak, M. (2003) 'Hyperidentities: postmodern identity patterns in massively multiplayer online role-playing games', in M. Wolf and B. Perron (eds), *The Video Game Theory Reader*. London, Routledge: 87–102.

Finn, M. (2001) *Console Games in the Age of Convergence*. Computer Games and Digital Textualities, IT University of Copenhagen, The Department of Digital Communication and Aesthetics.

Fiske, J. (1987) *Television Culture*. London and New York, Routledge.

Fiske, J. (1992) 'The cultural economy of fandom', in A. L. Lewis (ed.), *The Adoring Audience. Fan Culture and Popular Media*. London and New York, Routledge.

Fiske, J. and J. Watts (1985) 'Video games: inverted pleasures'. *Australian Journal of Cultural Studies* 3(1).

Flanagan, M. (2003) '"Next level" women's digital activism through gaming', in G. Liestol, A. Morrison and T. Rasmussen (eds), *Digital Media Revisited*. Cambridge, MA, MIT Press: 359–88.

Flichy, P. (1995) *Dynamics of Modern Communication. The Shaping and Impact of New Communications Technologies*. London, Sage.

Forfás (2004) 'Electronic games study'. Unpublished, internal report. Dublin, Forfás.

Frasca, G. (1999) 'Ludology meets narratology: similitude and differences between (video) games and narrative', *Ludology.org*.

Frasca, G. (2003) 'Simulation versus narrative: introduction to ludology', in M. Wolf and B. Perron (eds), *The Video Game Theory Reader*. London, Routledge: 221–35.

Friedman, T. (1995) 'Making sense of software: computer games and interactive textuality', in S. Jones (ed.), *CyberSociety: Computer Mediated Communication and Community*. California, Sage.

Fromme, J. (2003) 'Computer games as part of children's culture'. *Game Studies* 3(1).

Fuller, M. and H. Jenkins (1995) 'Nintendo and New World travel writing: a dialogue' in S. Jones (ed.), *CyberSociety: Computer Mediated Communication and Community*. Thousand Oaks, CA, Sage.

Funk, J. (2002) 'Video games grow up: electronic games in the 21st century', in V. Strasburger and B. Wilson (eds), *Children, Adolescents, and the Media*. London, Sage: 118–41.

Gailey, C. (1993) 'Mediated messages: gender, class, and cosmos in home video games'. *Journal of Popular Culture* 27(1): 81–97.

Gallagher, S. and S. H. Park (2002) 'Innovation and competition in standard-based industries: a historical analysis of the US home video game market'. *IEEE Transactions on Engineering Management* 49(1): 67–82.

Gansmo, H., J, H. Nordli and K. Sørenson (2003) 'The gender game. A study of Norwegian computer game designers', in C. MacKeogh and P. Preston (eds), *Strategies of Inclusion: Gender and the Information Society. Experiences from Private and Voluntary Sector Initiatives*. Trondheim, NTNU: 115–39.

Garnham, N. (2000) *Emancipation, the Media and Modernity. Arguments about the Media and Social Theory*. New York, Oxford University Press.

Gee, J. P. (2003) *What Video Games Have to Teach Us about Learning and Literacy*. New York, Palgrave Macmillan.

Gee, J. P. (2004) 'Learning by design: games as learning machines', *Gamasutra*.

Goodwin, J. (2001) *Fragging the Men: Quaking from a Woman's Perspective*. Joystick 101.

Green, B., J.-A. Reid and C. Bigum (1998) 'Teaching the Nintendo generation? Children, computer culture and popular technologies', in S. Howard (ed.), *Wired-Up: Young People and the Electronic Media*. London, UCL Press: 19–42.

Griffiths, M. (1991) 'Amusement machine playing in childhood and adolescence: a comparative analysis of video games and fruit machines'. *Journal of Adolescence* 14: 53–73.

Griffiths, M. (1997) 'Computer game playing in adolescence'. *Youth and Society* 29(2): 223–7.

Haddon, L. (1988) 'Electronic and computer games: the history of an interactive medium'. *Screen* 29(2): 55–7.

Haddon, L. (1993) 'Interactive games', in P. Hayward and T. Wollen (eds), *Future Visions: New Technologies of the Screen*. London, BFI: 123–47.

Haddon, L. and G. Paul (2001) 'Design in the IT industry: the role of users', in R. Coombs, K. Green, A. Richards and V. Walsh (eds), *Technology and the Market. Demand, Users and Innovation*. Northampton, MA, Edward Elgar: 201–15.

Haines, L. (2004) *Women and Girls in the Games Industry*. Manchester, Media Training North West.

Harries, D. (ed.) (2002) *The New Media Book*. London, BFI.

Harvey, D. (1989) *The Condition of Postmodernity: an Enquiry into the Origins of Cultural Change*. Oxford, Blackwell.

Hawkins, J. (ed.) (1987) *The Oxford Reference Dictionary*. London, Guild Publishing.

Hayes, D. (2004) 'Computer games should be taught in schools', *Evening Standard*, 26 October.

Herz, J. C. (1997) *Joystick Nation*. London, Abacus.

Hesmondhalgh, D. (2002) *The Cultural Industries*. London, Sage.

Holland, W., H. Jenkins and K. Squire (2003) 'Theory by design', in M. Wolf and B. Perron (eds), *The Video Game Theory Reader*. London, Routledge: 25–46.

Holmes, T. (2002) 'Art games and breakout: new media meets the American arcade', in F. Mäyrä (ed.), *Computer Games and Digital Cultures Conference Proceedings*, Tampere, Tampere, University Press. (Available at www.selectparks.net.)

Huizinga, J. (1949) *Homo Ludens: A Study of the Play-element in Culture*. London, Routledge & Kegan Paul.

IDSA (2001) *Economic Impacts of the Demand for Playing Interactive Entertainment Software*. Washington, Interactive Digital Software Association.

IGDA (2004) *Quality of Life in the Game Industry: Challenges and Best Practices*, International Game Developers Association.

Jansz, J. and R. Martis (2003) 'The representation of gender and ethnicity in digital interactive games' in M. Copier and J. Raessens (eds), *Level Up: Digital Games Research Conference*. Utrecht, Utrecht University Press: 260–9.

Järvinen, A. (2002) 'Halo and the anatomy of the FPS'. *Game Studies* 2(1).

Jenkins, H. (1988) 'Complete freedom of movement: videogames as gendered play spaces' in J. Cassell and H. Jenkins (eds), *From Barbie Dolls to Mortal Kombat: Gender and Computer Games*. Cambridge, MA, MIT Press: 262–97.

Jenkins, H. (1999) Testimony before the US Senate Commerce Committee.

Jenkins, H. (2002) 'Interactive audiences?' in D. Harries (ed.), *The New Media Book*. London, BFI.

Jones, S. (2003) *Let the Games Begin. Gaming Technology and Entertainment among College Students*. Washington, DC, Pew Internet and American Life Project.

Joyner, L. and J. TerKeurst (2003) 'Accounting for user needs and motivations in game design'. University of Abertay, Scotland, unpublished paper.

Juul, J. (1999) 'A clash between game and narrative. A thesis on computer games and interactive fiction'. MA thesis, Dept. of Digital Aesthetics and Communication. Copenhagen, IT University of Copenhagen.

Juul, J. (2001) 'The repeatedly lost art of studying games. A review of Avedon, E. and Sutton-Smith, B. (eds), *The Study of Games, 1971*'. *Game Studies* 1(1).

Juul, J. (2003) 'The game, the player, the world: looking for a heart of gameness', in M. Copier and J. Raessens (eds), *Level Up: Digital Games Research Conference*, Utrecht University, Utrecht.

Juul, J. (2004) 'Introduction to game time' in N. Wardrip-Fruin and P. Harrigan (eds), *First Person. New Media as Story, Performance and Game*. Cambridge, MA, MIT Press: 131–42.

Kellner, D. (2002) 'New media and new literacies: reconstructing education for the new millennium', in L. A. Lievrouw and S. Livingstone (eds), *Handbook of New Media*. London, Sage.

Kendall, L. (2002) *Hanging Out in the Virtual Pub. Masculinities and Relationships Online*. Berkeley, University of California Press.

Kennedy, H. (2002) 'Lara Croft: feminist icon or cyberbimbo? On the limits of textual analysis'. *Game Studies* 2(2).

Kent, S. L. (2002) *The Ultimate History of Video Games: From Pong to Pokemon*, Roseville, CA, Prima.

Kerr, A. (2002) 'Representing users in the design of digital games'. in F. Mäyrä (ed.), *Computer Games and Digital Cultures Conference Proceedings*, Tampere, University of Tampere Press.

Kerr, A. (2003a) 'The digital games industry in Ireland: current and future strategies'. Paper presented at Conference on Digital Games Industries: Developments, Impact and Direction, ESRC Centre for Research on Innovation and Competition (CRIC), The University of Manchester, 19–20 September 2003.

Kerr, A. (2003b) 'Girls just want to have fun.' in N. Oudshoorn, E. Rommes and I. van Sloten (eds), *Strategies of Inclusion: Gender in the Information Society Strategies of Inclusion: Gender in the Information Society*. Vol III: Surveys of Women's Experience. Trondheim, Centre for Technology and Society: 211–232.

Kerr, A. (2003c) '(Girls) Women just want to have fun: a study of adult female gamers'. in M. Copier and J. Raessens (eds), *Level Up: Digital Games Research Conference Proceedings*. Utrecht, University of Utrecht, Press.

Kerr, A. (2003d) 'Live life to the power of PS2. Locating the gaming industry in the new media environment'. *Irish Communications Review*, 9.

Kerr, A. (2004) 'Policies for the games industry in Europe: Competitive culture(s)?' Presentation at the Korean Games Conference, Seoul. Available from the author.

Kerr, A. and R. Flynn (2003) 'Revisiting globalisation through the movie and digital games industries'. *Convergence: The Journal of Research into New Media Technologies* 8(2).

Kerr, A., P. Brereton and J. Kücklich, (2006) 'New media: New pleasures?' *International Journal of Cultural Studies* 9(1).

Kerr, A., P. Brereton, J. Kücklich and R. Flynn (2004) *New Media: New Pleasures?* Final project report. Dublin, STeM.

KGDI (2004) *The Rise of Korean Games. Guide to Korean Game Industry and Culture.* Seoul, Korean Game Development and Promotion Institute.

Kinder, M. (1991) *Playing with Power in Movies, Television and Video Games.* Berkeley, University of California Press.

Kinder, M. (2002) 'Narrative equivocations between movies and games', in D. Harries (ed.), *The New Media Book.* London, BFI: 119–43.

King, G. (2002) 'Die hard/try harder: Narrative, spectacle and beyond, from Hollywood to videogame.' In G. King and T. Krzywinska (eds), *ScreenPlay. Cinema/videogames/interfaces.* London, Wallflower Press: 50–65.

King, G. and T. Krzywinska (2002a) 'Introduction: cinema/videogames/interfaces' in G. King and T. Krzywinska (eds), *ScreenPlay. Cinema/Videogames/Interfaces.* London, Wallflower Press: 1–32.

King, G. and T. Krzywinska (eds) (2002b) *ScreenPlay. Cinema/Videogames/ Interfaces.* London, Wallflower Press.

Kirriemuir, J. and A. McFarlane (2004) *Literature Review of Games and Learning.* London, NESTA futurelab.

Klastrup, L. (2003) 'You can't help shouting and yelling: fun and social interaction in super monkey ball' in M. Copier and J. Raessens (eds), *Level Up. Digital Games Research Conference Proceedings.* Utrecht, Utrecht University Press.

Kline, S. (1998) *Video Game Culture: Leisure and Play Preferences of British Columbia Teens.* Burnaby, BC, Canada, Media Analysis Laboratory, Simon Fraser University.

Kline, S., N. Dyer-Witheford and G. De Peuter (2003) *Digital Play. The Interaction of Technology, Culture and Marketing.* Montreal, McGill-Queen's University Press.

Kücklich, J. (2001) 'Literary theory and computer games'. Paper presented at COSIGN 2001 (Computational Semiotics for Games and New Media) Conference, Amsterdam, 10–12 September.

Kücklich, J. (2003) 'Perspectives of computer game philology'. *Game Studies* 3(1).

Kücklich, J. (2004) 'Other playings – cheating in computer games.' Retrieved 26/09/2005, available from www.itu.dk/op/papers/kuecjlich.pdf

Kushner, D. (2003) *Masters of Doom: How Two Guys Created an Empire and Transformed Pop Culture.* New York, Random House.

Lacey, N. (2000) *Narrative and Genre: Key Concepts in Media Studies.* Basingstoke, Macmillan.

Landow, G. (1997) *Hypertext 2.0.* Baltimore, MD, and London, Johns Hopkins University Press.

Laurel, B. (1993) *Computers as Theatre.* Reading, MA, Addison-Wesley Publishing Company.

Laurel, B. (2001) *Utopian Entrepreneur.* Boston, MA, MIT Press.

Lie, M. (1998) *Computer Dialogues: Technology, Gender and Change.* Trondheim, Centre for Women's Research, Norwegian University of Science and Technology.

Lievrouw, L. A. and S. Livingstone (2002) 'The social shaping and consequences of ICTs' in L. A. Lievrouw and S. Livingstone (eds), *Handbook of New Media.* London, Sage: 1–15.

Lindley, C. (2003) 'Game taxonomies: a high level framework for game analysis and design', *Gamasutra* feature article, 3 October.

Lister, M., J. Dovey, S. Giddings, I. Grant and K. Kelly (eds) (2002) *New Media: A Critical Introduction*. London, Routledge.

Livingstone, S. (2002a) 'What is media literacy?' *media@LSE*.

Livingstone, S. (2002b) *Young People and New Media. Childhood and the Changing Media Environment*. London, Sage.

Livingstone, S. (2003) 'Children's use of the internet: reflections on the emerging research agenda'. *New Media and Society* 5(2): 147–66.

Lumby, C. (1997) 'Panic attacks: old fears in a new media era'. *Media International Australia* 85: 40–46.

Machlup, F. (1984) *Knowledge: Its Creation, Distribution, and Economic Significance*. Princeton, NJ, Princeton University Press.

Mackay, H., (ed.) (1997) *Consumption and Everyday Life. Culture, Media and Identities*. London, Open University and Sage.

Mackenzie, D. and J. Wajcman (eds) (1999) *The Social Shaping of Technology*. Buckingham, Open University Press.

Mactavish, A. (2002) 'Technological pleasure: the performance and narrative of technology in *Half-Life* and other high-tech computer games', in G. King and T. Krzywinska (eds), *ScreenPlay. Cinema/Videogames/Interfaces*. London, Wallflower Press: 33–49.

Mactavish, A. (2003) 'Game mod(ifying) theory: the cultural contradictions of computer game modding'. Paper presented at the conference: Power Up: Computer Games, Ideology, and Play, held at the University of the West of England, Bristol, UK on 14–15 July.

Manovich, L. (2001) *The Language of New Media*. Cambridge, MA, MIT Press.

Marshall, F. D. (1997) 'Technophobia: video games, computer hacks and cybernetics'. *Media International Australia* 85: 70–8.

Marshall, P. D. (2002) 'The new intertextual commodity' in D. Harries (ed.), *The New Media Book*. London, BFI.

Marshall, P. D. (2004) *New Media Cultures*. London, Arnold, Hodder Headline.

Marvin, C. (1988) *When Old Technologies Were New. Thinking about Electric Communication in the Late Nineteenth Century*. New York, Oxford University Press.

McClean, H. (2004) 'Welcome to play school'. *Guardian*, 16 November.

McFarlane, A., A. Sparrowhawk and Y. Heald (2002). *Report on the Education Use of Games*. London, Department of Education and Skills and TEEM (Teachers Evaluating Educational Multimedia).

McLuhan, M. (1964) *Understanding Media*. London, Sphere Books.

Media Analysis Laboratory (1998) 'Video game culture: Leisure and play preferences of British Columbia teens.' Burnaby, Simon Fraser University.

Miège, B. (1989) *The Capitalisation of Cultural Production*. New York, International General.

Miles, I. and J. Gershuny (1983) *The New Service Economy: The Transformation of Employment in Industrial Societies*. London, Frances Pinter.

Moores, S. (1990) 'Texts, readers and contexts of meaning: developments in the study of media audiences.' *Media, Culture and Society* 12: 9–29.

Morley, D. and R. Silverstone (1990) 'Domestic communication-technologies and meanings'. *Media, Culture and Society* 12: 31–55.

Morris, S. (2003) 'WADs, Bots and Mods. Multiplayer FPS games as co-creative media', in M. Copier and J. Raessons (eds), *Level Up. Digital Games Research Conference Proceedings*. Utrecht, Utrecht University Press.

Morris, S. and D. Marshall (2000) 'Game'. *M/C: A Journal of Media and Culture* 3(5).

Mosco, V. (1996) *The Political Economy of Communication. Rethinking and Renewal.* London, Sage.

Moulthrop, S. (2004) 'From work to play: molecular culture in the time of deadly games', in N. Wardrip-Fruin and P. Harrigan (eds), *First Person. New Media as Story, Performance and Game.* Cambridge, MA, MIT Press: 56–69.

MPAA (2002) *2001 US Economic Review.* California, Motion Picture Association of America.

MPAA (2004) *2004 US Entertainment Industry: MPA Market Statistics.* California, Motion Picture Association of America.

Murray, J.H. (1997) *Hamlet on the Holodeck: the Future of Narrative in Cyberspace.* Cambridge, MA, MIT Press.

Murray, J. (1997) 'The pedagogy of cyberfiction: teaching a course on reading and writing interactive fiction', in E. Barrett and M. Redmond (eds), *Contextual Media. Multimedia and Interpretation.* Cambridge, MA, MIT Press: 129–62.

Neale, S. (1980) *Genre.* London, BFI.

Nelmes, J. (2003) *An Introduction to Film Studies.* London, Routledge.

Newman, J. (2002a) 'In search of the videogame player. The lives of Mario'. *New Media and Society* 4(3).

Newman, J. (2002b) 'The myth of the ergodic videogame'. *Game Studies* 2(1).

Newman, J. (2003) *Videogames.* London, Routledge.

Nordli, H. (2004) 'The gathering experience: a user study of a computer party,' in N. Oudshoorn, E. Rommes and I. Van Slooten (eds), *Strategies of Inclusion: Gender in the Information Society.* Vol. III: Surveys of Women's User Experience. Trondheim, Centre for Technology and Society: 319–335.

NPD Group (2005) 'First Quarter 2005 US Video Game Industry Retail Sales', NPD.

Nutt, D. and D. Railton (2003) 'The Sims: real life as genre'. *Information, Communication and Society* 6(4): 577–92.

O'Connor, B. and E. Klaus (2000) 'Pleasure and meaningful discourse. An overview of research issues'. *International Journal of Cultural Studies* 3(3): 369–87.

OECD (2004a) *Digital Broadband Content: Music.* Paris, OECD.

OECD (2004b) *Digital Broadband Content: The Online Computer and Video Game Industry.* Paris, OECD.

OFCOM (2004) 'Ofcom's Strategy and Priorities for the Promotion of Media Literacy'. A statement. London, Office of Communications.

O'Hagan, M. and C. Mangiron (2004) 'Games localization: When 'Arigato' Gets Lost in Translation'. Paper Presented at the New Zealand Game Developers Conference, Dunedin, New Zealand, University of Otago, 24 June.

Oudshoorn, N. and T. Pinch (eds) (2003) *How Users and Non-Users Matter. The Co-Construction of Users and Technology.* Cambridge, MA, MIT Press.

Oudshoorn, N., E. Rommes and M. Stienstra (2004) 'Configuring the user as everybody. Gender and design cultures in information and communication technologies'. *Science, Technology & Human Values* 29(1): 30–63.

Pham, A. (2001) 'Video game firms power up; amid sector's consolidations craze, a contest of survival intensifies', *Los Angeles Times.*

Poole, S. (2000) *Trigger Happy: the Inner Life of Videogames.* London, Fourth Estate.

Poremba, C. (2003) 'Patches of peace: tiny signs of agency in digital games', in M. Copier and J. Raessens (eds), *Level Up: Digital Games Research Conference Proceedings.* Utrecht, Utrecht University Press.

Postigo, H. (2003) 'From *Pong* to *Planet Quake*: post-industrial transitions from leisure to work'. *Information, Communication and Society* 6(4): 593–607.

Prensky, M. (2001) *Digital Game Based Learning.* New York, McGraw-Hill Education.

Preston, P. (2001) *Reshaping Communications. Technology, Information and Social Change.* London, Sage.

Preston, P., A. Kerr, and A. Cawley (2003) 'Skills Requirements of the Digital Content Industry in Ireland'. Unpublished preliminary report. Dublin, FAS Skills Labour Market Research Unit.

Provenzo, E. F. (1991) *Video Kids. Making Sense of Nintendo.* Cambridge, MA, Harvard University Press.

Ray, S. G. (2004) *Gender Inclusive Design. Expanding the Market.* Hingham, MA, Charles River Media.

Rideout, Victoria, J., U. Foehr, D. Roberts, M. Brodie (1999) 'Kids, media and the new millenium.' Menlo Park, Henry J. Kaiser Family Foundation.

Roe, K. and D. Muijs (1998) 'Children and computer games. A profile of the heavy user'. *European Journal of Communication* 13(2): 181–200.

Ryan, M.-L. (1999) *Cyberspace Textuality. Computer Technology and Literary Theory.* Bloomington, Indiana University Press.

Ryan, M.-L. (2001) *Narrative as Virtual Reality. Immersion and Interactivity in Literature and Electronic Media.* Baltimore, Johns Hopkins University Press.

Salen, K. and E. Zimmerman (2003) *Rules of Play. Game Design Fundamentals.* Cambridge, MA, MIT Press.

Schatz, T. (1993) 'The new Hollywood', in A. Collins (ed.), *Film Theory Goes to the Movies.* New York, Routledge.

Schleiner, A.-M. (2001) 'Does Lara Croft ware fake polygons: gender analysis of the 1st person shooter/adventure game with female heroine and gender role subversion and production in the game patch'. *Switch* (switch.sjsu.edu/web/v4n1/annmarie.html).

Schott, G. and K. Horrell (2000) 'Girl gamers and their relationship with the gaming culture'. *Convergence* 6(4): 36–53.

Schott, G. and M. Kambouri (2003) 'Material plane: interactivity in social play with computer games.' *Convergence* 9(4): 41–54.

Screen Digest (2001) 'Interactive leisure software: market assessment and forecasts to 2005'. *Screen Digest*, June.

Screen Digest (2002) 'Media dominate UK leisure time. Biggest increase in media use was in past three years'. *Screen Digest*, April.

Screen Digest (2004) 'Interactive leisure software report: Global market assessment and forecasts to 2007', *Screen Digest* on behalf of the Entertainment Software Publishers Association (ELSPA).

Sefton-Green, J. and D. Buckingham (1998) 'Digital visions: children's "creative" uses of multimedia technologies', in J. Sefton-Green (ed.), *Digital Diversions. Youth Culture in the Age of Multimedia.* London, UCL Press: 62–83.

Shamoon, E. (2005) 'Everything you need to MMO'. *Game Developer*, April.

Sheff, D. (1993) *Nintendo's Battle to Dominate an Industry.* London, Hodder & Stoughton.

Silverstone, R. (1999) 'Play' in *Why Study the Media?* London, Sage: 59–67.

Silverstone, R. and L. Haddon (1996) 'Design and the domestication of information and communication technologies: technical change and everyday life', in R. Mansell and R. Silverstone (eds), *Communication by Design. The Politics of*

Information and Communication Technologies. Oxford, Oxford University Press: 44–74.

Silverstone, R. and E. Hirsch (eds) (1992) *Consuming Technologies. Media and Information in Domestic Spaces*. London, Routledge.

Skillset (2004) *Employment Census 2004: The Results of the Fifth Census of the Audio-Visual Industries*. London, Skillset.

Skirrow, G. (1986) 'Hellivision: an analysis of video games' in C. MacCabe (ed.), *High Theory/Low Culture. Analysing Television and Film*. Manchester, Manchester University Press: 115–42.

Sørensen, K. (2002) 'Social shaping on the move? On the policy relevance of the social shaping of technology perspective', in K. Sørensen and R. Williams (eds), *Shoping Technology, Guiding Policy: Concepts, Spaces and Tools*, Cheltenham, Edward Elgar.

Søtamaa, O. (2004) 'Playing it My Way? Mapping the agency of modders'. Paper presented at Internet Research 5.0 Conference, University of Sussex, UK, 19–22 September.

Southern, M. (2001) 'The cultural study of games: More than just games'. Paper presented at the Game Developers Conference Europe in London.

Spectrum Strategy Consultants (2002) *From Exuberant Youth to Sustainable Maturity. Competitiveness Analysis of the UK Games Software Sector*. London, Department of Trade and Industry (DTI).

Squire, K. (in press). '*Civilization III* as a world history sandbox'. Available online at Website. education.wisc.edu/kdsquire/research.html. Accessed January 2006.

Squire, K. D. and S. Barab (2004) Replaying history: engaging urban underserved students in learning world history through computer simulation games'. *Proceedings of the 2004 International Conference of the Learning Science*. Los Angeles, UCLA Press.

Stewart, K. and H. Choi Park (2002) *PC-Band Culture: a Study of Korean College Students' Private and Public Use of Computers and the Internet*. Seoul, International Communications Association.

Sutton-Smith, B. (1997) *The Ambiguity of Play*. Cambridge, MA, Harvard University Press.

Swalwell, M. (2003) 'Multi-player computer gaming: Better than playing (PC Games) with yourself.' *Reconstruction* 3(4). Available online at www.reconstruction. ws/034/swalwell.htm

Takahashi, D. (2002) *Opening the XBox: Inside Microsoft's Plan to Unleash an Entertainment Revolution*. Roseville, CA, Prima Publishing.

Taylor, T. L. (2002) '"Whose game is this anyway?' Negotiating corporate ownership in a virtual world', in F. Mäyrä (ed.), *Computer Games and Digital Cultures, Conference Proceedings,* Tampere, Finland, Tampere University Press.

Taylor, T. L. (2003a) 'Multiple pleasures: women and online gaming'. *Convergence: The Journal of Research into New Media Technologies* 9(1): 21–46.

Taylor, T. L. (2003b) 'Power gamers just want to have fun? Instrumental play in a MMOG', in M. Copier and J. Raessens (eds), *Level Up. Digital Games Research Conference Proceedings*, Utrecht, Utrecht University Press.

TerKeurst, J. (2002) *Games Are Like Fruit. Japanese Best Practice in Digital Game Development*. Report of a Department of Trade and Industry International Technology Service Mission. Dundee, IC CAVE, University of Abertay Press and DTI.

TerKeurst, J. (2003) *Creativity is Not Enough. Global Best Practice in Digital Game Publishing.* Report of a Department of Trade and Industry International Technology Service Mission to North American and France. Dundee, IC CAVE, University of Abertay Press and DTI.

Tschang, T. (2003) 'Beyond normal products and development processes: computer games as interactive experiential good and their manner of development'. Paper presented at What Do We Know about Innovation? A conference in honour of Keith Pavitt, Freeman Centre, University of Sussex, UK.

Turkle, S. (1984) *The Second Self. Computer and the Human Spirit.* New York, Simon & Schuster.

Turkle, S. (1997) *Life on the Screen: Identity in the Age of the Internet.* London, Phoenix.

Van der Graaf, S. and D. B. Nieborg (2003) 'Together we brand: America's army', in M. Copier and J. Raessens (eds), *Level Up. Digital Games Research Conference Proceedings,* Utrecht, Utrecht University Press.

Vered, K. O. (1998) 'Blue group boys play *Incredible Machine,* girls play hopscotch: social discourse and gendered play at the computer', in J. Sefton-Green (ed.), *Digital Diversions. Youth Culture in the Age of Multimedia.* London, UCL Press: 43–61.

Wark, M. (1994) 'The video game as emergent media form'. *Media International Australia* 71: 21–30.

Wasko, J. (1994) *Hollywood in the Information Age: Beyond the Silver Screen.* Oxford, Polity Press.

Wayne, M. (2003) 'Post-Fordism, monopoly capitalism, and Hollywood's media industrial complex'. *International Journal of Cultural Studies* 6(1): 82–103.

Webster, F. (1995) *Theories of the Information Society.* London, Routledge.

Williams, D. (2002) 'Structure and competition in the US home video game industry'. *The International Journal on Media Management* 4(1): 41–54.

Williams, D. (2003) 'The video game lightening rod: constructions of a new technology 1970–2000' in *Information, Communication and Society* 6(4): 523–50.

Williams, R. (1974) *Television: Technology and Cultural Form.* London, Fontana/ Collins.

Williams, R. (1981) *The Sociology of Culture.* Chicago, University of Chicago Press.

Williams, R. (1997) 'The social shaping of information and communication technologies', in H. Kubicek, W. Dutton and R. Williams (eds), *The Social Shaping of Information Superhighways.* Frankfurt, Campus Verlag.

Winston, B. (1996) *Technologies of Seeing: Photography, Cinematography and Television.* London, BFI.

Winston, B. (1998) *Media, Technology and Society. A History: From the Telegraph to the Internet.* London and New York, Routledge.

Wolf, M. (2001) *The Medium of the Video Game.* Austin, University of Texas Press.

Wolf, M. and B. Perron (eds) (2003) *The Video Game Theory Reader.* London, Routledge.

Woodcock, B. (2005) 'Market Share by MMOG'. Available online at www.mmogchart.com/ Accessed 10 May 2005.

Woolgar, S. (1991) 'Configuring the user: the case of usability trials', in J. Law (ed.), *A Sociology of Monsters. Essays on Power, Technology and Domination.* London, Routledge: 58–97.

Wright, J. C., A. C. Huston, E. A. Vandewater, D. S. Bickham, R. M. Scantlin, J. A. Kotler, A.G. Caplovitz and J. Lee (2001) 'American children's use of electronic media in 1997: a national survey'. *The Journal of Applied Developmental Psychology* 22: 31–47.

Wright, T. and P. Briedenbach (2002) 'Virtual violence, social meaning and gender: competition and cooperation between FPS Game Players'. Paper presented at the conference on Challenge of Computer Games, Lodz, Poland, in October 2002.

Wright, T., E. Boria and P. Briedenbach (2002) 'Creative player actions in FPS online video games'. *Game Studies* 2(2).

Yates, S. J. and K. Littleton (1999) 'Understanding Computer Game Cultures.' *Information, Communication and Society* 2(4): 566–83.

Yoon, S. (2000) 'Computer games and the culture of young people in Korea'. Paper presented at the IAMCR conference in Singapore, on July 17–20.

INDEX